PRAISE FOR

Ross Heaven's
The Sin Eater's Last Confessions

"I can heartily recommend this book to anyone
interested in healing or Celtic traditions as an engrossing
and entertaining read, a moving biography of a powerful,
wise, and humble man."

—Lauren D'Silva, *BellaOnline*'s New Age editor

"A moving memoir ... Highly recommended for anyone
interested in Celtic lore and shamanism."

—*New Age Retailer*

✦ ✦ ✦

❖ About the Author

Ross Heaven is the director of the Four Gates Foundation, one of Europe's leading organizations for the teaching, promotion, and application of spiritual wisdom and freedom psychology. He offers workshops in healing, empowerment, techniques of self-awareness, and indigenous wisdom.

He is also a Western-trained therapist and an award-winning author of several books on shamanism, healing, and personal development, including *Darkness Visible*, *Plant Spirit Shamanism*, *Love's Simple Truths*, *The Way of the Lover,* and *The Sin Eater's Last Confessions*, which is the prequel to *Walking with the Sin Eater*. He has also produced *Infinite Journeys*, a trance drumming tape that can be used as an accompaniment to the shamanic journeys described in these books.

As well as the shamans and sin eaters of Wales, Ross has worked extensively with the healers of the Amazon and Andes and offers sacred journeys to work with them and the ayahuasceros and San Pedro shamans of Peru. For details of these trips and a free information pack (or for other information about Ross and his work in general), email ross@thefourgates.com or visit him online at www.thefourgates.com.

Walking
WITH THE
Sin Eater

A Celtic
Pilgrimage on
the Dragon Path

Ross Heaven

Llewellyn Publications
Woodbury, Minnesota

FIRST EDITION
First Printing, 2010

Book design by Rebecca Zins
Cover design by Lisa Novak
Cover image © age fotostock/SuperStock

Llewellyn is a registered trademark of Llewellyn Worldwide, Ltd.

Library of Congress Cataloging-in-Publication Data

Heaven, Ross.
Walking with the sin eater : a Celtic pilgrimage on the dragon path / Ross Heaven.—1st ed.
    p.   cm.
  Includes index.
  ISBN 978-0-7387-1916-0
  1. Magic, Celtic—Wales. 2. Shamanism—Wales. 3. Spiritual life. 4. Sin. 5. Heaven, Ross.
I. Title.
  BF1622.C45H43 2010
  299´.16—dc22

2009036604

Llewellyn Publications
A Division of Llewellyn Worldwide, Ltd.
2143 Wooddale Drive, Dept. 978-0-7387-1916-0
Woodbury, MN 55125-2989, U.S.A.
www.llewellyn.com

Printed in the United States of America

For my children,
Mili, Jodie, Ocean, and Javen:
May the world support you and love you as I do.

And for our newest plant spirit babies, Freddy and Kai.

In memory of my father and mother.

Contents

Contents

Disclaimer

The techniques, recipes, and approaches in this book are for interest purposes only. The exercises presented here have been tested in many real-life applications, and no harm has ever arisen as a result (most people have benefited enormously). It is important, however, to act sensibly and responsibly when undertaking spiritual or emotional discovery work of any kind. It is also important that you double-check all formulas and recipes given in this book for legality and safety before using them internally or externally and, if you are in any doubt about any of these practices or recipes, that you take medical or other advice to reassure yourself that there are no contraindications.

Any application of these exercises is at the reader's own risk, and the author and publisher disclaim any liability arising directly or indirectly from them, their use, or the recipes described in this book.

Sinners and Pilgrims

> MAN IS A creature who walks in two worlds and traces upon the walls of his cave the wonders and the nightmare experiences of his spiritual pilgrimage.
>
> *Morris West,*
> *novelist and playwright*

IN *Funeral Customs: Their Origin and Development* (1926), the historian Bertram Puckle described sin eaters as "abhorred by the superstitious villagers as a thing unclean" and remarked that "the sin-eater cut himself off from all social intercourse with his fellow creatures by reason of the life he had chosen; he lived as a rule in a remote place by himself, and those who chanced to meet him avoided him as they would a leper. This unfortunate was held to be the associate of evil spirits, and given to witchcraft, incantations and unholy practices."

That, however, was not entirely my experience.

In the mid-1960s—now almost half a century ago; how strange it is to be part of time!—I was a young boy and moved with my family to a village called Ullingswick in the English county of Herefordshire, close to the border of Wales. It was an odd and timeless place, distant from the glosses of modern life, where the world turned differently. Nature held dominion, like a force or a feeling that rippled with the wind among the grasses of its fields, producing the curious sensation that the village itself was somehow a manifestation of spirit rather than a community made and intended by man. It was as if its real purpose was to provide a doorway to the otherworlds that a shaman would recognize, and this doorway was always open.

The spirits passed freely through this portal, so that everything was alive with their presence and rich in symbol and metaphor. The people who lived among them, guided by their whispers, conducted themselves according to a different rhythm and way of seeing the world, so that coincidence, ancient practices, and magical beliefs had become part of the village fabric. Anything else—any purely rational approach or appeal to science, for example—was likely to be looked upon with suspicion or dismissed with a shake of the head and a kindly smile, as if a gentle rebuke was being offered to someone who did not yet know better.

Newly arrived from the city, I was at first that someone; but as the years passed, and I breathed in the spirits around me and their ancient magic carried on the country air, I began to see the world through their eyes, too, and to understand a different order of truth.

"The setting is not far from my home in Mid Wales, just over the English border, and I could easily picture this sleepy village," commented Lauren D'Silva, editor of *BellaOnline*, while reviewing the book I wrote about my experiences in this curious landscape of spirit.[1] "Even now the pace of many Herefordshire villages feels several decades behind that of modern towns." Those who know the county agree that there is something unusual or even unearthly about it.

The book that D'Silva comments upon is called *The Sin Eater's Last Confessions*. In it, I write about my experiences with Adam, a man I was to meet by following the trail of coincidence and the whisperings of spirit that were an ever-present voice in Ullingswick.

Adam had been a sin eater in Wales during his own youth, and some of Buckle's descriptions were apt of him. He did indeed live "in a remote place by himself." His cottage stood at the edge of the village, alone and isolated from the rest of the community, and it had long fallen into disrepair, with a lopsided architecture that had begun to take on the form of the land itself. It stood at

---

1   The review appears at http://www.bellaonline.com/articles/art27080.asp (accessed September 14, 2009).

a crossroads, just back from the lane, surrounded by tall bushes and trees and fronted by a tangle of blackthorn and briars. It had an atmosphere or personality of its own, like the fairytale cottage of a witch: something almost alive.

Puckle says of the sin eater that "those who chanced to meet him avoided him as they would a leper," and this is also true. Adam appeared to have few friends and spent most of his time alone—apart, that is, from the villagers who would call on him in secret for the healing only he could offer them.

Far from being "the associate of evil spirits, and given to witchcraft, incantations and unholy practices," sin eaters were accomplished healers—we might today call them shamans—who knew the ways of the soul: what it is, how we might learn its true intentions, and how sin can shape and corrupt it, as well as how to restore it through spiritual practice and the powers of confession, plants, rituals, and omens.

As D'Silva writes: "There is a great deal of wisdom in Adam's methods of healing. He had a wonderful understanding of plant remedies and ... many of his teachings can be recognized as shamanic ways of understanding the world, which are found to agree from culture to culture."

I shared a friendship with Adam for more than ten years, and some of these healing secrets were passed to me. *The Sin Eater's Last Confessions* is a record of their passing.

In the early 1980s, however, I returned to the village after a time away at university and, seeking out my old friend once more, I came instead upon a mystery: Adam's cottage, his garden, and Adam himself were nowhere to be found.

The author and minister Frederick Buechner wrote in one of his meditations on the search for truth that "in one way or another, man comes upon mystery as a summons to pilgrimage." And so it was for me. To find my friend, or at least solve the riddle of what had become of him, I embarked on a new journey of discovery. *Walking with the Sin Eater* is the story of that adventure, one that was taken ostensibly in search of Adam but really, I know now, in search of myself.

Although it is a sequel of sorts, it also stands alone as a testament to what I found and to the ways in which pilgrimage may reveal to us the workings of our soul. Throughout this book I will not burden you with references to my previous book, but it is a work you may also wish to read if your interest is piqued by the practices I describe here, and doing so will undoubtedly provide you with a fuller understanding of the sin eater's art.

What we call the beginning is often the end
And to make an end is to make a beginning.

T. S. Eliot,
"Little Gidding"

1

The Field

Creator Spirit, by whose aid
The world's foundations first were laid...
From sin and sorrow set us free
And make thy temples worthy Thee...
And, lest our feet should step astray,
Protect and guide us in the way.

John Dryden,
"Veni, Creator Spiritus"

ONE OF THE most moving events I have ever witnessed took place nearly thirty years ago now, in an ordinary field in Wales. Quiet and unassuming, the event I have in mind was not a grand and mournful episode but a simple expression of loss, yet there must be a lesson in it, because I remember it so clearly, and events that touch our hearts like this can surely never be trivial.

I had traveled to Wales some weeks after returning to the sleep-filled Herefordshire village of Ullingswick, where I had spent my childhood and where I had first met Adam, the elderly sin eater who had taught me the Celtic ways of spirit.

I had not long graduated from university and had been restless and uncertain about the choices now facing me, and I believed that Adam could help me with the questions I had about my future. He had, after all, taught me years before that we must walk a Path of Purpose in order to know the mission of our souls and so we do not lead aimless lives or become caught in a web of lies, which for most people, he said, is the reality of the world. I had returned to the village hoping that Adam would help me refine my purpose and find my direction in life, but instead I found him gone.

Nobody seemed to know where he was, and I had resigned myself at first to allowing the universe this mystery. Some things, after all—as Adam had often said—are not meant to be understood by the mind but engaged with by the soul. In time, then, the essence of these mysteries may flower and emerge in some subtle way to add meaning to our lives through their poetry and magic and the deeper truths that run through them.

Reflecting on his words at the time, I had come to regard his disappearance as a symbol, another of his initiations into the nature of our human condition. For without Adam to guide me, I would have to stand alone—as we all must, having come to this world to find our ways and allow our souls to grow and fill with knowledge.

Still, I was a young man, and there was a part of me, too, that yearned for adventure and to solve the riddle that Adam had become. That part began to speak most loudly during the next few weeks and to reel me in by presenting this particular mystery as a quest, like those Adam had spoken of that ran through the myths and legends of Wales: a sacred challenge that might reveal the meaning in a life.

The answers the Welsh heroes found on their own quests often raised further questions, of course, because there can never be an absolute end to searching until our time here is finally spent. That, however, was not the point: the adventure itself provided the nourishment for their souls that they needed, and through it they came to understand themselves a little better. That same understanding was what I needed now.

And so, whether hero-inspired or as a confused young man looking for the guidance of an elder, I resolved that Adam's disappearance was more than a vanishing act; it was a final gift he had left me: a possibility for new wisdom.

I had few clues about where to start: a pot of ashes containing the remains of the many confessions that Adam had heard over the years and a stone dish that he had used to burn herbs and incense during his healings, both of which I had discovered on the empty land where his cottage once stood. But these were of little use to me in discovering his whereabouts now.

As I mulled it over during the next few days, though, a strange energy began to captivate me as I realized that there were other trails to follow. The most promising of these was that I had met some of Adam's friends—significantly Cad, whose home I had visited in Wales. It was many years ago now and I had not kept in contact with Cad since then, but at least I knew where he lived and how to find him. It was this thin thread that had led me to Wales.

On my arrival at his cottage, however, no one had been home, but I had anticipated as much. I would, after all, be arriving unannounced, so I could not expect Cad to be waiting for me or even to recognize me when we met, so I had brought a tent and a few provisions in case I might need them, and set up camp in a field adjacent to his house.

Cad's cottage was different than Adam's. The sin eater's had been a tumbling whitewashed affair, lopsided and falling into the arms of nature, whereas Cad's was solid and brick-built. It stood back from the road on a slight elevation, and beyond and around it the fields took on a steeper incline, rising up to a hilltop that never quite completed itself but folded at its peak like a wave and rolled gently down into the valley below. A stone wall and a green-painted picket fence guarded the front of his house, unlike the unruly hedge of briars that had surrounded Adam's garden. The only similarity between the two houses, in fact, was that they both stood at a crossroads: in Adam's case, a meeting of four ways; in Cad's, a meeting of three, just off-center from where two roads joined and formed a T.

I had been camping for two days, awaiting Cad's return from whatever business had taken him. The field that had become my temporary home was used for grazing sheep, but they are cautious animals, and most of the time they stayed on the hills and grassland above me, keeping a wary distance from the stranger in the field below.

It was on the morning of the third day that the event took place that was to have such a subtle but present impact on me.

A sheepdog entered the field. It looked badly injured and was limping as it struggled to make its way across the grass, but it was determined to do so, even when it began dragging itself more than walking. It made it almost to the middle of the field and then lay down, unable to go any farther, as if coming home to do no more than die.

The sheep had no doubt regarded this dog as their enemy or jailer for years as it rounded them up and controlled them. I had a vision of them scattering in panic whenever the dog ran towards them at the bidding of a shepherd. But now they watched in still silence.

They began to move closer then, abandoning their safe places, and formed a circle around their old adversary, still without sound. A few moved closer still and began to nudge it, as if willing the dog to stand and take on its familiar role.

When it could not, in unison they started to bleat, like they were praying for it or offering words of encouragement and healing.

Then, all at once, their prayers ended, and an eerie silence fell upon the field. Even the birds stopped singing. The dog was dead.

After a few moments, during which nothing moved and no sound could be heard, the sheep began their mournful cries again, but gentler and more quietly now, like a low keening for a friend who was lost.

And the wolf shall dwell with the lamb.

ISAIAH 11:6

I saw then that animals are not so different from us. We take people for granted, as the sheep had this dog. Those we regard as enemies we distance from ourselves, perhaps more from habit than genuine fear or distaste, and it is only when they are gone that we realize how they have shaped us and how, in one way or another, we needed them so we could define who we are.

Adam had spoken of a crucial hour, a time when opportunity can be grasped and a change can be made to overcome our habitual ways of seeing and doing so that a greater truth can be found. This crucial "hour" could arise, in fact, at any moment in a life and was an opportunity to be grasped, he said. But perhaps the real crucial hour in anyone's life is the moment before death, when the meanings of our pasts are finally revealed. The dog had crawled into this field to make its peace and say its farewells to the sheep whose lives had been so entwined with its own, and the sheep had shown it affection and acknowledged the understanding between them in these, its dying moments. Perhaps they realized that they were not enemies at all, but relied on each other, because there was a greater force which controlled them both: the shepherd, whose will they all had followed.

The sound of a car startled me from my reflections, and looking to my left, I saw an old Morris Minor pull up at the house. When I looked back, the sheep were gone, and only the dog remained.

I wanted to do something—to make some sort of gesture for the dog as an act of respect because of what had passed between us in its dying moments. So, turning away from the car, I walked over to the dog, knelt at its side, and began to pray for it.

Almost without thinking, I found that my eyes narrowed as I entered the attitude of gazing that Adam had taught me: a way of spirit-vision, as he called it, which enabled us to sense and connect with the soul. By doing so, I could see the sheen of life that still surrounded the dog. Its soul was a shadow now, as if a thin blanket of light had been laid over its body, its essence gathering itself for its journey back to the world of spirit.

I willed my energy to enter it so I could shape the soul within it, creating an umbilicus from the threads of light I pulled from its body, just as I had seen Adam do when he had been the sin eater at the funeral of a friend years before.

I looked up, and other threads of energy began snaking down into the field from the sky and, reaching up, I wove them into the umbilicus I had created. Once the two were joined, the dog's soul would find its way to whatever Heaven dogs go to—the same as ours, I suspected, since energy does not discriminate; it is formless and shapeless, as Adam had described it, and would return to the same source, or "cloud of awareness," that we all come from.

The church once believed (and perhaps still does) that animals—and all things on Earth—were put here by God in the service of human beings, so there was no real difference between a dog and any other "object." Animals had no souls or emotions but were automata, like clocks. They could not be hurt because they had no feelings, and if they made a noise when they were "damaged," it was not because they felt pain or sorrow or loss; it was simply a sound like a clock would make if it fell to the floor and was broken.

It is a strange view that seems at odds with the Bible, a book which Adam had often quoted (although he taught that we should "choose our passages carefully" when reading it), so I had become reasonably familiar with its contents. A few lines from Ecclesiastes now crossed my mind:

> *Man's fate is like that of the animals; the same fate*
> *awaits them both: As one dies, so dies the other.*
>
> *All have the same breath ... All go to the same*
> *place; all come from dust and to dust all return.*
>
> *Who knows if the spirit of man rises upward and if*
> *the spirit of the animal goes down into the earth?*
>
> ECCLESIASTES 3:19–21

I knew, because I had just watched the spirit of this dog rise towards the sky, following a thread of energy that had purposefully sought it out from above.

This is the difference between words and actions in "the field of deeds," as Adam had called our lives: by following the words or beliefs of others—even if they are accepted religious "truths"—and repeating those words or acting upon them without question, we become automata. By testing them through our experiences, however, we discover a deeper truth.

My work finished, I stood up and looked back towards the house and the car beside it. The man who had driven it was watching me with curiosity. I couldn't make out his features because of the distance between us, but that was unimportant because I knew who he was. I began walking towards him.

He did not seem surprised to see me, even though it had been five or six years since we had last met, and then only fleetingly. The fact that he knew me and that introductions were unnecessary was clear from his words. "I expected you here a lot sooner. Still, it's good to see you. Come in."

And with that, he waved me into his house through a front door that had been unlocked all the time he was away.

Traditionally the Celts are a courteous, trusting, and hospitable people, although the relationship between the Welsh and the English had become strained in the 1970s. An angry faction had grown up and begun to burn the homes of English people who had moved to Wales and to demand separation from the rest of the British Isles. Indolent youth had become infected with this anti-English sentiment and, when I was a young man in Hereford, it was almost guaranteed that an army of teenage thugs would break the borders on weekend nights to look for trouble in the English streets.

It seemed odd to me then, and does now, that they should demand the English leave them alone and then go looking for a fight across the borders with people who were doing just that. But bored young men with warrior blood will always need challenges and causes to fight, even if they make no sense. The battle itself and the initiation it offers are themselves the prizes.

There was still a lot of anti-English feeling in Wales in the 1980s and, although I felt safe enough with Cad, I was conscious that I was a stranger in his country, with an accent that would cast me as an enemy.

Cad, however, was welcoming. He made tea and we chatted awhile, catching up on the events of our lives and what we had been doing since we last met. Eventually, and naturally enough, the conversation turned to what had brought me to Wales, although I suspected he already knew the answer to that from the way he had first addressed me. He had anticipated my arrival at some point; that was clear enough.

"Ah, yes, Adam," said Cad. "I saw him before he left."

"So you know where he is, then?" I asked.

"Where he is ... no. Not where he is now. I last saw him three years ago."

Three years. My mind drifted back to what I had been doing three years ago, away at university, learning about new cultures and old practices during my studies of psychology and anthropology. All of the cultures we had looked at—"primitive societies," we would call them—were untouched by Western ideologies and so had something in common: a belief in the soul, the power of nature, reciprocity, and a spirit that guides all things and can visit us in dreams and flashes of truth.

Many times during my studies I had been reminded of the adventures I had shared with Adam and of his beliefs, which were in many ways similar to those of the cultures I was studying. Adam had called his own practices the "old ways," and through our work together, I had come to see them not as quaint and outmoded but representative of a fundamental reality and wisdom that ran beneath the glosses of the world and offered us important lessons about our lives and purpose ... if we chose in our hearts to let them.

"But I know where you are going," Cad said suddenly. "I have something for you, you see ... a gift from Adam. He asked me to give you this, should you ever come this way."

Chance and destiny. Adam had spoken of these two forces in our lives as well, and how they were connected. He had left me a gift. That was a purposeful act. But was it chance or destiny that brought me here to receive it?

He could never have known for certain that I would return to the village where I grew up, for example, or look for him when I found that he was gone—or that I would make a journey to Wales as a result of this. It was more likely, in fact, that I would take a job, settle down, or travel once I had completed my degree, as young men usually do. It was chance, really, that had brought me home, and a chance meeting with Cad several years before that had allowed me to follow this trail back to the Welsh hills.

Or was it? Hearing now that Adam had left something for me, my sense of things changed. Whatever I was about to be given had taken on an air of destiny, as if there could have been no other outcome. There are moments, then, when chance and inevitability are woven together, and it is in these moments that we spin our destinies from the cloth we are handed by fate.

Cad turned away and opened a drawer on a nearby dresser. He pulled something from it and passed it to me. It was a journal. Adam's journal.

It felt strange to be holding it, knowing that Adam's words—his personal reflections and thoughts—would be within it and that he had left them for me ... stranger still since it was not at all what I would have expected a journal of Adam's to be.

He had always seemed a very "proper" man to me—very British (although he was proud of his Welsh blood and would not have thanked me for saying that)—and, through his teachings and way of life, the holder of some deep and arcane knowledge. I had no idea that he had kept a journal, but if I had, I would have imagined it to be some ancient, leather-bound tome smelling of libraries and learning, and containing secrets written in the antique script of some lost code, like you might find in a museum or a monastery.

But it was an ordinary spiral-bound notebook, the sort that costs pennies in any stationers. The pages were stained with age and dirt, as if he had from time to time received some vision while working in his garden and written his thoughts down quickly with still-dirty hands. How typical of him to bring nature into his philosophy, I thought—tangibly and physically in the soil on the pages and, here and there, the flowers and cuttings he had pasted onto them. I opened it at random towards the end and read the entry there.

◆ ◆ ◆

The same dream again. I am standing in a meadow near a tall and odd-shaped hill which has a castle or a church at its top—really, it is a gateway, I think, but I must make the climb to find out.

A dragon path snakes its way to the summit, which will make the climbing easy. Lines of energy, like mist, circle the hill, from the sky down to where I stand.

I know what this dream means: The earth requires my presence. It is time for me to go.

I know where this hill is too. I have seen it before in dreams, and I have a memory of it from somewhere else.

The moon is high and white, casting a silver light through the mist, but it is daytime too and the sun is up: a curious mixture of light and shade, a crucial hour, no doubt, which is neither day nor night.

I remember the words of a stranger from long ago: that we are food for this moon unless we lead a life of purpose. Perhaps the day and night represent a choice then: between purpose and nothingness, and this is another sign that I must leave the things I know.

It seems to me that there are many times when a pilgrimage may be useful to settle the mind and restore the soul, but certainly there are two: when a man is first starting out in life and needs to know his path, and when he is nearing the end of it and must recollect his deeds, weigh them in the balance, and understand the path he has walked.

Well, I am not a young man anymore! So the purpose for me in making this journey cannot be in question. My pilgrimage will be the telling of my life and a gathering of power. It means that things are coming to an end.

I have a curious feeling in my dream, as well: as if someone is watching me, standing behind me, and observing my journey—that they have been following me for days, though I cannot see them.

Another stranger? Or perhaps I am the stranger now?

8B

◆ ◆ ◆

I smiled when I read it. I had bombarded Adam with questions for years. He had accepted this with good grace, although he rarely provided direct answers, preferring that I find them for myself through the wisdom of the natural world, the country walks he had insisted we take, and the teachings he had imparted along the way. When he first began writing this journal, he could not have intended anyone but himself to read it, but towards the end, when he had decided that he would pass it on to me, he must have known that an entry like that would raise a thousand questions.

I wondered if he'd deliberately phrased it to be as vague and enticing as possible so as to further pique my interest. I could imagine the twinkle of the trickster in his eye as he wrote about a "choice between purpose and nothingness" and "things coming to an end." Did he mean a literal end or a change of some other kind? And, in either case, having decided to pass his journal to me, where, I wondered, did I fit in? Surely, a man of purpose like Adam had a thought-through plan for his actions.

"He said you'd have questions," said Cad, before I had a chance to ask anything. "He also said that I was to provide no answers, and you should know what to do."

Seeing my puzzled look, he added: "You have only to ask the cattle for them to instruct you, and the birds of the sky for them to inform you. The creeping things of the earth will give you lessons, and the fish of the sea provide an explanation. There is not one such creature but will know that the hand of God has arranged things like this."

I knew the words from the Bible, although I didn't recognize the passage,[1] but I understood the instruction implicit within them: that nature would provide my answers.

A number of years before, Adam had shown me how to read signs and omens in nature by entering a dreaming state—a place of betwixt-and-between, he called it—and by absorbing what the landscape, the plants, and the animals—"the creeping things of the earth"—had to tell me. Hearing Cad's words now, I looked out of the window to the fields beyond, remembering what Adam had taught me.

"Yes," said Cad. "Nature has our answers ..."

I left the journal on the table and walked out into grassland and sun.

---

1   Job 12:7–10

2

Messages Written in Cloud

Over earth and ocean, with gentle motion
This pilot is guiding me
Lured by the love of the genii that move
In the depths of the purple sea

Percy Bysshe Shelley,
"The Cloud"

THE ANCIENT CELTIC practice of taking guidance from nature is called *rhamanta* and relies on our surrender to chance and destiny. In its simplest form, it means holding a question in mind and walking out into fields and forests with a desire only to be led by the whispers of spirit. The flight of birds across a valley, the play of sunlight on leaves, or even a gust of wind might then become significant and provide the answers we are looking for, since, as Adam had explained it, "nature is the visible face of spirit: a way of connecting with intelligent forces who know far more than we do."

It is not always as easy as it sounds, however, because we have been taught to use logic, not spirit, to gain knowledge from the world. The rational mind will usually try, therefore—and often with some success—to dismiss the signs we are given as irrelevant or nonsensical.

That is why the practice is combined with others to quieten a mind that can sometimes be an enemy and not an ally to this work. Foremost among these is a walk of attention, which is really a moving meditation and involves deep, slow breathing, slow steps, and allowing the eyes to go slightly out of focus as you walk. It is better to keep the eyes on the ground and the awareness in the belly, in fact, as if you are being pulled across the land by some invisible force that connects to your solar plexus, so you do not feel as if you are guiding yourself at all. This combination of actions produces an almost trancelike state, where the deeper stirrings of spirit can be more clearly perceived.

Adam had taught that it is best to look for three signs—or, rather, allow these signs to find us—so we can check the information each provides against the others and then assemble all three creatively to reveal a final answer.

My slow walk now took me to a bank of grass on which three small trees were growing and where I could lie down, my back against the soft bank in the shelter of their branches, to gaze into the sky. I held the position for several minutes, deepening into the silence around me and attuning myself to the rhythms of the world.

A few wisps of cloud drifted in an otherwise serene and cloudless sky, and the branches of the trees creaked softly as they moved in a breeze so slight it was almost not there. I grew more relaxed, hypnotized by the gentleness of the day, and at first didn't notice anything remarkable in the sky above me.

As I watched more closely, though, a single larger cloud drifted into view, framed by the branches of the trees as if they were cupped hands holding it delicately, almost in prayer. It had an odd shape, more rounded at the top, with a thin, trailing wisp at its base like the stem of a glass or goblet, or perhaps a rose. It shifted its shape as I watched it, finally reassembling itself and becoming more mounded and hill-like before it dissolved into the blue that surrounded it and vanished.

In the play of tree and sky, I considered that two omens had been revealed: the chalice or hill-like cloud and the prayerful branches that held it. I wasn't consciously seeking a third, but as I sat up, I happened to look across the meadow, and my eyes momentarily came to rest on a gateway that led into the field.

For some reason it held my attention, although it felt less significant as a sign than the others. But then I remembered Adam's words in the journal I had read: "I am standing in a meadow near a tall and odd-shaped hill which has a castle or a church at its top—really, it is a gateway, I think."

Perhaps that was the significance of the gate: to confirm that the hill in Adam's vision really was a doorway or a portal of some kind and that, in order to find him, it was a gateway that I should be looking for.

The final stage in Adam's teachings of how to receive signs from nature was to put all three symbols together and create one singular piece of information from them, like a story which flowed from you.

My question, of course, had concerned Adam's whereabouts and how he could be found. Really, I was looking for some significant landmark, or guidance about a first step I could take on my journey towards his discovery. Putting these three signs together and arriving at the "story" of what I had been shown, it didn't seem to amount to very much; really, it was a single phrase:

> *There is a gateway that leads to a chalice and a*
> *hill. Adam will be found by passing through it.*

I had made the pieces fit, but, in truth, it didn't feel as if the information I had gathered was very useful or even very new, since Adam had already written in his journal about hills and gates.

For me, perhaps the least useful of the signs was the gate. It raised as many questions as it answered: If it was a real gate, where was it? Where did it lead? And, most importantly, how could it be found? After all, there must be a million gates in a million fields throughout Britain, many of them, no doubt, on hills like this one where I now sat, so

I still had no real sense of where to look or how to begin. My question—Where has Adam gone?—remained unanswered.

"That is because you are not a Welshman—unfortunately for you," said Cad when I joined him again in the kitchen and related what I had seen. "If you knew your Welsh history, you would now know exactly where to look, and you would realize that the most important of all the signs you were given was the gateway itself!"

"Why?" I asked. "What is significant about a gate in a field?"

"It is not the gate but the symbol that is important," he replied. "*Pa gur yv y porthaur?* 'What man is the gatekeeper?' Do you know the answer to that question?"

I must have looked completely blank, and so, smiling to himself, he continued: "*Pa gur yv y porthaur?*—What man is the gatekeeper?—is a poem in the Black Book of Camarthen—*Llyfr Du Caerfyrddin*—the earliest surviving manuscript entirely written in Welsh.

"The name of the book comes from its association with the Priory of Good Saint John in Camarthen and, to state the obvious, because it is bound in black. It was written in AD 1250, and among other things it tells the stories of Arth and Myrddin—better known to you, I imagine, as King Arthur and Merlin.[2]

"The poem is a dialog between Arthur and the gate-keeper of a fortress he wishes to enter, in which Arthur—*Penteyrnedd yr Ynys hon*, the overlord of Wales—recounts the deeds of he and his men.

"The point is this: that to pass through the gateway—or to the next stage of life, if you will—there must be a reca-pitulation or confession—the telling of a life, as Adam put it in his journal—and there must be worth in what we have so far achieved. If not, we shall not pass but be turned away to make atonements before we can try again.

---

2   The Welsh word *arth* (or art) means "bear," and *ur* means "man." Putting them together produces *art-ur*, or "bear-man," a reference to the courage and power in battle of the great warrior who was later to become known as Arthur. The character of Merlin (Myrd-din), meanwhile, first appears in Geoffrey of Monmouth's *Historia Regum Britanniae* (History of the Kings of Britain) in AD 1136 and is an amalgam of two legendary figures: Myddrin Wyllt (Merlinus Caledonensis), a prophet, sage, and madman, and Aurelius Ambro-sius, a war leader. From these sources, Geoffrey produced the char-acter he called Merlin Ambrosius, who was born of a mortal woman but sired by an incubus, from whom he inherited his magical pow-ers. In fact, "The Merlin," according to some, is not a character at all (composite or otherwise) but a title, or rank, given to Celtic wizards of great ability.

"So now you have your three symbols: the chalice-hill, the praying hands of the tree, and the gateway through which Arthur passed ... do you know now where Adam may be found?"

An answer began to form itself for me, but before I could speak, Cad grew impatient. "It should be obvious to you," he said. "Adam wrote that he wishes to be a pilgrim—and where do you suppose a Welshman would make a pilgrimage to? Karnack ... Delphi ... Jerusalem? Of course not! He would look only to one place: *Annwn* ... Avalon ... the holy Isle of Apples ..."

"Glastonbury," I said.

"Precisely!" said Cad. "Glastonbury indeed! The resting place of Arthur and one of the stations of the Grail, or sacred chalice. A place interwoven with the long history of the Welsh, and the only place on Earth besides Wales that a true Welshman might pilgrimage to!"

I felt like a poor student who was being told off by his teacher, but then Cad softened. "Don't feel bad that you didn't work it out or find the answer quick enough," he said. "It might have taken me longer too, but I had a little help ... Adam told me where he was going!"

"So you knew all along?" I exclaimed.

"Well, yes, I did," said Cad, "but I wanted to see what you knew and how well Adam had taught you. You didn't do badly, as it happens, when you were out in the fields."

I felt a little uncomfortable hearing that I had been tested when I didn't even know a test had been set—and by someone I didn't know that well, either, but I reminded myself that although Adam's style was different from Cad's, he probably would have done the same: encouraged me to find answers for myself from a world teeming with information.

Anyway, I thought to myself, I wouldn't have to put up with Cad's tests any longer, because now that I knew where Adam had gone, I could take my leave whenever I wished, and—*if* I wished—make a journey of my own to Glastonbury in search of him.

I realized in that moment, however, that although I hadn't consciously decided to take such a journey, wishing had nothing really to do with it, because my soul had already chosen a path of adventure. The mystery of Adam was too thick and the words in his journal too intriguing and resonant of my own quest for direction for me to ignore the signs I had been given and turn my back on Glastonbury.

"There are many times when a pilgrimage may be useful to settle the mind and restore the soul," Adam had written, "but certainly there are two: when a man is first starting out and needs to know his path, and when he is nearing the end of it and needs to recollect his deeds."

I was starting out in life and needed to know my path— it was what had brought me back to Hereford in the first place, and then to Wales and to Cad—but was I ready to make a pilgrimage?

A single word from Cad snapped me out of my reverie. "We leave in the morning," he said.

"We?"

"Yes," he said, "I'm coming with you ... at least part of the way."

My thoughts went back to the events of the morning, which now seemed such a long time ago. The dying dog, my sense of its life and death entwined with that of the sheep, each of them led by a force greater than themselves that they had overlooked in their relationship to each other, for weren't they both really controlled by the shepherd, even though they thought themselves to be free?

I glanced at Cad, who had turned away from me to make tea. Which of us was the dog and which the sheep, I wondered, because I had no doubt that in this field, Adam was shepherd to us both.

A passage from the Bible went through my mind:

> *You were like sheep going astray*
> *But now you have returned to the*
> *Shepherd and Overseer of your souls.*

1 PETER 2:25

It was true. I had been going astray—or, at least, I was not clear in my path. Now I had a destination, although little idea where, outside of physical geography, my journey would take me next.

3

Wormholes and Dragon Paths

Curiosity does,
No less than devotion,
Pilgrims make.

Abraham Cowley,
English poet and essayist
(1618–1667)

THE NEXT DAY started dark. Fog clung to the hillsides in thick strands and was denser in the hollows of the land, as if they were basins holding a grey-white broth.

Not even the sun shone through. In the watery sky there was a pale spotlight only, obscured by curtains of chilled mist, which gave an emotional coldness to the world as well as a physical one.

I went to work dismantling my tent, which was wet with dew and fog, while Cad took a shovel to the field and buried the dog that had come there to die. Then we waited for the weather to lift and the sun to warm the land.

It never quite did, though, and so, despite a reasonably early start to the day, it was only in the afternoon that we decided to leave, having abandoned all hope of setting out in anything other than sheets of still, grey fog.

Cad's car, although ostensibly green, looked as if it had not been washed for years, and instead of factory bright-ness, it had taken on the colors of the lands it had driven through. Shades of brown caked its sides where it had caught the mud from country lanes, and leaves of various hues, from rust to lime, had worked their way into the fenders and the treads of the tires. It looked either camouflaged or like a living, organic thing more than a machine. I wondered if this was deliberate and remembered that Adam had never much cared for the man-made either. "Metal trying to be trees," he had muttered one day while looking out over the valleys to a range of pylons beyond. I loaded my belongings into the back of Cad's 'organic car' and climbed into the passenger seat next to him.

"At this time of day, in these conditions, and in this old car, we can be sure that we will arrive in Glastonbury and certain that it will not be today," said Cad.

"But then, had we risen before dawn, had the day been perfect for travel, and were we driving a shiny new Aston Martin ... we would still not get there today! We are not just driving to a place picked at random from a map, you see; we are making a pilgrimage—a considered journey to a holy land—and we must approach our travel in a reverent and reflective way, as befits such an enterprise.

"There are places of power along our route that I wish to show you as well—places where we must say our prayers and seek blessings, so our journey inevitably will be slow. I estimate that you will arrive at your destination in three days. I hope that is satisfactory?"

It was fine. Three days was not such a long time, and I had nowhere else to be, in any case. I sat back for the drive, and as we set off, I pulled Adam's journal out of my pack so I could re-read the message of yesterday and think again about the questions it had raised.

As I flicked through the book, however, I came first to another entry that seemed more appropriate to the journey that, consciously or otherwise, I had committed myself to.

◆ ◆ ◆

Pilgrimage. The word is from peregrinus *(Latin), which means "foreign." This, in turn, comes from* peregre—*"going," or, I believe, "to go."*

It arises in turn from two other words: per *(through) and* ager *(field). The very root of the idea, then, is this: "To journey through fields"... to enter the garden of nature again.*

The absolute goal of the pilgrimage, however, is not to go further and further afield but to return home—to arrive back where we started. It is not a one-way journey but a circle that completes itself.

The point, along the way, is to open our eyes ... to change ourselves because of the mission we have undertaken and the visions it affords us ... so we see ourselves once more in "the Garden," not just afield. A pilgrimage is not an act of abandonment and refusal, therefore, but of embracing and atonement. It is not a "running away from" but a "running towards"...

Every pilgrimage takes place in the betwixt-and-between: the point between departure and return. Any action might therefore be a pilgrimage, whether the journey takes a moment or a lifetime—because we are always acting. To be pilgrims is what we came to this world to do. It is our destiny, and chance can only intercede if we allow it.

The difference between the two—chance and destiny—is intent. When we are clear on our actions and commit to them fully, there arises a Total Act: a decisive movement by which we call to destiny and direct it so our lives become what our souls intended.

> *If you came this way,*
> *Taking any route, starting from anywhere,*
> *At any time or at any season,*
> *It would always be the same:*

You would have to put off
Sense and notion. You are not here to verify,
Instruct yourself, or inform curiosity
Or carry report. You are here to kneel
Where prayer has been valid ...
Here, the intersection of the timeless moment
Is England and nowhere. Never and always.[3]

It doesn't really matter where our pilgrimages take us, as long as they have meaning for us. The timeless moment is what pilgrims seek—the place beyond sense and notion.

We wish to stand in the presence of God and, as His shadow descends on us, to see that He holds a mirror. Then we can return to the home we left and know that our sins are forgiven ... because we forgave them in ourselves.

8B

◆ ◆ ◆

The same curious mark finished the entry, as it did in the first one I had read. In Adam's handwriting, it looked like an ampersand (&) followed by a capital *B*.

---

3   T. S. Eliot, "Little Gidding" (*Four Quartets*, Harcourt, 1943).

"Do you know what this is?" I asked Cad.

"It seems to be a pilgrim mark," he said, taking his eyes briefly off the road.

"Those on a journey of the soul often carry such a sign as proof of their pilgrimage and for protection along the way. When they reach their destination, they might then carve the mark near the shrine they are visiting as evidence of their journey and to absorb some of the power and grace of whatever holy thing is there. The design represents, in effect, the mark of a pilgrim's soul, and by carving it, the spirit of the traveler blends with the spirit of that place and receives its benefactions and blessings.

"That mark"—he pointed to the ampersand—"is a lemniscate, one of the most powerful of magical symbols.

"In plain script, it would look like the number 8: two circles that meet at the center and wrap around each other. It stands for the meeting of souls: saint and sinner, man and God as one.

"You will often see similar marks on the staffs of healers. The caduceus—or Wand of Hermes—for example, is the emblem of God's messenger: the conductor of souls, carrier of prayers, and protector of certain tradesmen—notably, merchants and thieves (if you make a distinction between the two)!

"The symbol also appears on the staff of Asclepius, the lord of healing and medicine, where the 8 is made from two snakes twined in the form of a helix and adorned with wings so they become flying serpents: dragons."

"So it is a mark of healing, then?" I asked.

"Healing and protection, yes, but more importantly, of direction and purpose. It means that its bearer can never be lost because the circles double back on each other. By following them, the traveler may therefore go as far as he wishes into the worlds of spirit and matter but always find his way home.

"As for the other mark—the B—I would imagine that it represents Adam's true name. Sin eaters and healers often take a magical or sacred name, which connects them with nature and protects them from the Devil. But you know that, of course. I have never been told Adam's true name, but you were, I think?"

He was referring to the time in Wales when I had spent a night in the "cave of a dragon" as a form of ritual purification. Adam and Cad had both been there, keeping vigil outside, and in the morning, Adam had taken me to one side and revealed his true name to me: B*****.

We had then chosen a "true name" for me. "It is to save you from the Devil," Adam had said. "Now, if you ever find yourself standing before the old goat on a day of judgment, he will never find your true name in his register, but only your given, or Christian, name—and that will not help him at all!"

Reflecting now on that night in the dragon cave, I was reminded of something Adam had written in the first journal entry I had read: that on the hill in his dream there was a "dragon path" that snaked its way to the summit. I turned to the page again and asked Cad what it meant.

"What is a dragon path?" He smiled. "There are many answers to that question—the first of which is to look around you, because you are already on one!

"Some say they are the trails of dead men or places that spirits haunt, but really they are threads of energy that link one place or soul to another.

"The world, as you know, is not a simple matter and bears little resemblance to the way we *think* things are. Beneath everything we know—or think we know—there is a web of energy that holds our reality together and exists beyond the visible world. A dragon path is a particular thread in that web that will lead us to someone or something—a place, a person, or a passage in time—with which we have some business because we share something in common: a mood or a taste or, more likely, a sacred purpose.

"The thread you are following connects you to Adam. Precisely how is for you to discover, but it will certainly be because you are both looking for something, and the quest you are on unites you. So this is a dragon path you have created together. You sensed it when you arrived in Hereford and followed its trail to Wales, walking in Adam's footsteps—or, rather, in the threads of his energy. Through it, you found your way to me, just as he did when he visited me and left his journal for you. You sensed it again when you held that journal and in the field when you took counsel from nature and allowed its signs to guide you.

"Adam did not, after all, write down where he was going or invite you to join him, and I did not immediately reveal his destination; but somehow, still, you discovered it. You are here now, if you like, at the invitation of the clouds, and because you saw ripples in the threads of reality, one of which you have chosen to follow.

"There was an element of chance in your decision, of course, because, truly, there are millions of such threads all around us, and you could therefore have picked any one, but destiny also led you to the one you have chosen—or, at least, it is your destiny *now*!

"The Welsh are a poetic people, and we speak of the world in myth, but what we know is literal and factual too.

We say that there are tunnels beneath the earth that are the crawling spaces of dragons and serpents: the great worms.

"They are *worm*holes, in other words ... and you know what wormholes are, I take it? They are shortcuts through time and space.

"Scientists think they invented them," he laughed. "They use the analogy of a worm on an apple who, under normal circumstances, would take quite a while to navigate its sphere and arrive at the other side. But if an inspiration occurred to it and it bored through the apple's center ... well, how much quicker and easier its journey might be. It is the same for us: those who travel dragon paths pass through a wormhole, which, in their case, leads to the other side of the universe."

"You believe in such things, then?" I asked. "In the tunnels and travel through time? You are saying such things exist?"

He pondered the question for a moment. " 'Reality' and 'what really exists' are odd concepts," he said finally. "What is 'real' except what we experience as real? There are as many ways, then, to 'explain' dragon paths as there are to experience them, but the 'correct' explanation is only the one that has meaning for you.

"Let me say first that they are a pathway or a bridge to those people and places we feel most at home with, who have wisdom to impart to us, power to give us, or who can strengthen our purpose and sweeten our journeys. What attracts us to them is not physical but a mood, an emotion, or an affinity we have for them. It is, in other words, a sense of the purpose we share. They teach us more about who we are.

"If we develop this sense by becoming aware of the subtle forces around us, we therefore find a shortcut to a rich and more fruitful life. If we do not hone our senses, however, it will take us longer to get where we wanted, and our paths may seem harder and less 'juicy.' We will be the worms on the apple who, without inspiration, are trying to find our ways. We may still get there, but our efforts will be greater and there is more chance that we will get lost.

"Now let me answer your question in a different way and say that a dragon path is also a ley line: a roadway of energies that crosses the land. Those sensitive to the passing of dragons have always walked these paths, built their landmarks, monuments, and towns on them, and made trade on the routes they provide.

"There is no compulsion to follow ley lines, of course, but people have done so throughout history because they have found meaning in them, and they have also noticed that those who stray from them encounter problems in their lives. It is best, therefore, to stick to what is known—even if it is, in some ways, unknown!"

The idea of ley lines was familiar to me, partly because Adam had explained the concept when I was a child and partly because the term itself had been coined by a Herefordshire man, Alfred Watkins.

Watkins was born in January 1855 at the hotel his father owned: The Imperial, on Hereford's Widemarsh Street. His family was rich by country standards, and Alfred was provided with the finest schooling the county could offer. It was an education through which, he would say later, he learned "absolutely nothing," for, like most Herefordians, Watkins was practical and down-to-earth, in tune with the rhythms of nature, and in no way an academic who enjoyed study for its own sake.

He was highly intelligent and innovative, though, introducing the town to a number of new ideas, including the installation of a dynamo, which gave Hereford its first electric light, and, later, the invention of a pocket calculator used in photography (another of his passions). It was employed, amongst other things, to take the photographs for Scott's famous Antarctic expedition in 1910, the year when Watkins was also awarded the Progress Medal for his work.

Some of his other ideas were less successful, however, and some were downright eccentric. He was, for example, a founder of the Herefordshire Beekeepers Association and believed that bees had mystical powers. He provided the Association with a horse-drawn "bee van" that trundled along the lanes instructing those who would listen in the art of beekeeping and the use of bees in magic.

The esoteric world is blessed with geniuses, but it is also beset by as many oddballs as there are twigs to a great tree, and perhaps bee magic was not Watkins' finest hour. But better ideas were to follow.

In 1926, he formed the Old Straight Track Club to research one such idea received in a vision while he was walking a Herefordshire hillside. From his elevated position, he noticed that the landscape for miles around was crossed by routes that were marked along their way by churches, standing stones, and other landmarks that seemed linked by invisible lines of force. These he called "old straight tracks," or ley lines: threads of power that have drawn men to them throughout history. The Old Straight Track Club continued until the mid-1940s, and its records are now preserved in Hereford's city library, along with Watkins' photographs and glass-plate negatives.

Watkins died in 1935 at the age of eighty. The *Hereford Times*, in its obituary of April that year, described him as "intense, abrupt, hurrying to some business or engaged in animated conversation, oblivious to anything save the object in hand ... First and foremost he was a Herefordshire man, as native to the county as the hop and the apple."

With his passing, Watkins bequeathed a legacy. Before his death, in rapid succession he published *The Ley Hunter's Manual*, *Early British Trackways*, and his most famous work, *The Old Straight Track*, which explain his theory of ley lines, today so well established that it is regarded as obvious by those who know the land. These ley lines—or messages from the earth—were, in one sense, the dragon paths that Cad was referring to.

What sparked my imagination more was Cad's reference to wormholes. In science, they are linked to the idea of parallel universes, or multiverses—portals to alternate realities and other dimensions—where, right now, each of us may also exist as a double of ourselves in a slightly (or considerably) different form.

In a parallel universe, for example, a dirt-poor farmer might be a cash-rich millionaire ... or a president, priest, or panhandler. Apart from that change in status or occupation—or in hair color, shoe size, or the house they lived in—they would be the same person as us, and both of us would be alive right now, living the same lives in different universes alongside each other, oblivious to the existence of the other except for flashes of déjà vu or information received from dreams and visionary experiences, where these universes blend or collide and we may meet ourselves.

Some scientists even believe that multiple realities are possible in our own dimension, on this Earth that we know. Every moment is a decision point, they say, and every decision we make, however slight, changes the nature of the world around us. Neither the fate of a man nor the fate of a universe is predetermined, therefore, because every second forks into a Y-shaped moment where decisions are taken and our lives go in one way or another depending on the choices we make.

Even apparently trivial decisions can make a difference that is profound. The swatting of a fly might save the world, for example, if it was carrying a disease that would otherwise have killed a president. The abolition of slavery, the moon landing, or the invasion of a country may never have happened if that fly had lived. Indeed, the world itself might no longer exist.

Alertness to purpose and the more subtle nature of destiny's essence around us is therefore vital, because through it we have the ability to make conscious decisions that are sometimes of monumental, though easily missed, importance. This is what Adam had meant when he spoke of a "crucial hour"—really a series of crucial moments—where every action we take changes the world as a whole.

I looked down at the journal on my lap and read Adam's words again—that "any action we make might be a pilgrimage, whether the journey takes a moment or a lifetime—because we are always acting … The point, along the way, is to open our eyes … to change ourselves …

"The difference is intent: to be clear on our actions and commit to them with purpose."

Through the journey we take and the opportunity it gives us to rediscover or reinvent ourselves, perhaps we do, in some way, enter a parallel universe—one where we become new people through the choices we make. In that sense, at least, a dragon path really was a wormhole into another dimension of being.

I HAD DRIFTED off to sleep, "lost in wonder at the strangeness of the world," as Adam had once said about me—

before adding the word "unfortunate" to describe this flaw he saw in my character.

When I opened my eyes again, it was late afternoon and we were stopped at the side of a road. Fields surrounded us, and in one of them Cad was completing the work of putting up two tents.

I watched him for a while, thinking how different he was to Adam in both character and looks. Adam would be a very old man by now, and though he was hardly frail (and there was no reason, anyway, why a man of any age should not make a pilgrimage if he chose), I had some concerns for him. Cad, on the other hand, gave me no such worries. He was younger than Adam, stockier, and had a strength that came from the land and the elements.

His personality was an odd mixture, though: brusquer and less gentle, but more philosophical than Adam and perhaps better-read. I could never have imagined Adam talking about wormholes and parallel universes, for example. If he had wanted to make a point, it would more likely have been illustrated by the qualities of a particular plant or tree.

To be honest, I wasn't entirely sure that I even liked Cad, but that could just have been because I didn't know him that well. He was pleasant enough, but he had a certain impenetrability to him. Although I was grateful for the lift, for example, I wasn't quite sure why he had offered it or what we were doing now in this field. I made a note to myself that I would be more open after this and try to know him better.

I walked over to join him, passing an area of woodland to the left of what appeared to be our camping grounds for the night. "Welcome back!" he said, catching sight of me. "It was getting late, and I thought we needed a rest—the car most of all! I suggest we make camp here and continue our journey tomorrow."

We were just outside a village near Bath in the southwest of England, which meant that we had been on the road for four or five hours. Now evening was falling, although the day itself was still bright, the fog that had surrounded us in Wales having long ago vanished into the winds.

Bath is a city with a mythical past of its own. To the Celts, its thermal spring was a shrine to Sulis, the mother goddess, whose bubbling waters arrived from the tunnels beneath the earth, carrying underworld gifts of healing, prophecy, and the knowledge of other realms.

The Romans, arriving later, identified Sulis with Minerva, their virgin goddess of warriorship, poetry, wisdom, and medicine. Whether for matters of politics or as an acknowledgement of her greater supernatural powers, the Romans continued to regard Sulis as the primary goddess, however, and her spirit gave rise to their name for the city: Aquae Sulis—"the waters of Sulis." Archeologists have recovered prayers to the goddess scratched into metal and thrown into her sacred spring by penitents and those seeking power. There were others, too, called curse tablets, which were invocations for bad fortune to fall on enemies.

The Romans withdrew from the town early in the fifth century, and the baths they had made at the healing springs fell into disrepair—that is, until Thomas Guidott, a writer, "doctor of physik," and alchemist, moved to the town in 1668 to set up a medical practice. His *Discourse of Bathe*, about the curative properties of the waters, brought its spring back to life through the attentions of the aristocracy, who started to arrive there as a consequence and partake in the healing of Sulis. With that, the fortunes of Bath and the powers of the goddess both began a resurgence.

Cad was leaning on a shovel, the same one I'd seen him use earlier to bury the sheepdog. I hadn't noticed him pack it and assumed that he must have thrown it in the trunk of the car when I was dismantling my tent.

"There is another reason besides rest for our camping here, away from towns and people," he said, "something that Adam asked me to do if you should ever try to find him.

He would like to have done it himself, but the opportunity never arose. We have such an opportunity now, though."

"What is it?" I asked.

"Oh, nothing to worry about," said Cad, laughing. "It is a trifling matter, really.

"He asked me to kill you. That's all."

4

The Tunnels
Beneath the Earth

All places are alike,

And every earth is fit for burial.

Christopher Marlowe,
English dramatist
(1564–1593)

ARE YOU FAMILIAR with the works of John Dunne?" Cad asked, continuing his sentence after his previous announcement as if nothing unusual had ever been said. "Not the preacher and poet of Welsh descent, but John William Dunne, the soldier and engineer?"

I knew John Donne, the "preacher and poet." Strangely enough, I had even studied him during my degree and stayed for a while in a university hall of residence that was named after him. He was actually an English metaphysical poet, born in 1572, who died in 1631 having lived his entire life without setting a foot in Wales, as far as I was aware. His father, though (also called John), was of Welsh descent, and any link to Wales, I had learned—however tenuous or even non-existent—was all that any Welshman needed to turn a poet into a friend and compatriot. Adam had even tried to persuade me once that the American poet Ralph Waldo Emerson must at least have been "a Welshman at heart" based solely on his love of nature.

Donne had similar interests to Emerson, as it happened. The literary critic John Dryden, not a particular fan of Donne's work, summed up his style as "verses where nature only should reign" and commented that he "perplexes the minds of the fair sex with nice speculations of philosophy when he should engage their hearts and entertain them with the softnesses of love."

I had not heard of John William Dunne, "the soldier and engineer," however, and so Cad began an explanation.

"Some years ago, Mr. Dunne, a fighter in the Boer War, began to have dreams of events yet to happen, which, on waking, he found either to *be* real, or he would observe reality change over the next days and weeks until the events he had dreamed *became* real.

"He dreamed that his watch had stopped at a certain time, for example, and woke to find that it had. He also had dreams of greater significance—among them, of an earthquake and volcanic eruption on the island of Martinique and a fire in Paris, both of which came true.

"Mr. Dunne took to writing down his dreams and persuaded his friends to do the same. They were often amazed to find that reality accommodated their dreams very well, just as it had Dunne's, and gave them accurate descriptions of events that were yet to unfold.

"And so Mr. Dunne began to wonder about the nature of a world where things like this could happen. Certainly, it was not the world that we are taught to believe in, where time and reality have a nice, clean linear pattern, but one where future, past, and present are a single moment, eternal and swirling about us in an infinite and ongoing Now ... a world where distinctions of time are no more than the descriptions of the mind and bear little resemblance to what is actually real.

"Based on his experiences and the evidence of his experiments, Mr. Dunne arrived at the only conclusion he could: that there *is* no time, but rather, in sleep, dreams, and reveries, our souls wander freely and make contact with other dimensions where all that *can* be *is*, and everything that has, will, or could ever happen is open to influence and change through the agencies of chance and destiny.

"Suppose you dreamed the death of a loved one, for example, and, not wishing this to happen, of course, willed that the next night you would dream of that death averted. Then, through your Total Act and expression of power, that death would never take place. Or perhaps, that is, your *conscious* dreaming would lead you to another dimension, along a dragon path or through reality's wormhole, to a place where your loved one was still alive and well, even though she had perished in the reality you had left. Where would you then be: in this dimension or the next? The answer is neither and both, because the 'next' dimension would still be your dimension, and any dimension you occupy is always 'this one'!

"It is a conundrum, is it not? One which is solved by this simple fact: that we exist on two separate levels, inside and outside of time all at once, and the reality we experience is simply the one we choose.

"What this also means, of course, is that we are immortal, since calendars and clocks cannot hold us. There is no time.[4]

"In a way, what Dunne discovered was what Mr. Aquinas[5] found in his own revelations about a god who is everpresent in nature, seeing all things—past, future, and current—in the Now of a single, eternal moment, like a watchman looking down on the world from a wondrous tower and observing every event from a magical viewpoint.

---

4   Dunne wrote about his experiments in time travel in his book *An Experiment with Time* and of his theory of immortality in *Nothing Dies* and *The New Immortality*.

5   That is, Saint Thomas Aquinas (1225–1274), also known as Doctor Angelicus and Doctor Universalis. Aquinas was the first and foremost proponent of natural theology, a philosophy that regards God not as distant from humanity but omnipresent in the physical world, whose plans and designs are revealed through nature. He is considered the model teacher for the priesthood and the Catholic Church's greatest philosopher.

"What Dunne showed us through his experiments is that we are the watchmen ... or, to put it another way, that we exist in eternity like gods. Cast your mind back to a funeral we attended in Wales, for example, where Adam was the sin eater and you were the witness.[6] Your role there was to observe and ensure that the ritual was correctly performed, because no ordinary mourner may look upon a sin eater. But you had another job, too, although you may not have known it then: you were the watchman who saw the soul of the dead return to God, just as you saw the soul of a dog received back into Heaven when you prayed for it in the field on the day we met again. Through such observations, the witness bears testimony to immortality and is able to say that we exist beyond space and time, now and forever.

"To perceive events outside of time," he continued, "Mr. Dunne felt that we must seek out environments where our consciousness can be freed to allow what dreams may come. Later, these dreams are to be placed alongside the events of the world so we gather evidence for our abilities as time-travelers and seers.

---

6   This event is recorded in *The Sin Eater's Last Confessions*.

"And so we come to this," he concluded. "Your death. For, when we die, we stand truly outside of time and our spirit is free of the body forever."

I still knew little about Cad and had no idea if I had ended up in a field with a madman who was really planning my murder. I was grateful, therefore, when he added—almost as an afterthought, although he might have realized its importance to me—"I do not mean your literal death, of course, since you would have little to learn from that. I have in mind instead a technique that is offered to some initiates by their teachers, and to be more exact, it is a rebirth more than a death.

"It involves your burial to bring you closer to the spirit of the earth, but you will still be quite alive and able to breathe, I assure you, and, I imagine, more comfortable than I, since I will be your witness tonight and watch over you until the rising of the dawn. So, let me reassure you, this will not be a death but a living funeral, where you will only be buried alive."

Amusing as it is now to reflect on Cad's easy words and the lack of importance he obviously attached to the possible traumas of "only" being buried alive, the idea of it at the time filled me with less than enthusiasm, as you might imagine.

Burials like these, however, as I now know, are not just Celtic in origin but, as some of my studies have shown, classical and cross-cultural shamanic practices for receiving nurturing, healing, and advice from the earth. The idea is that the initiate "dies" to his old self by entering the grave that he digs and, once inside, he finds that it is not a grave at all but a womb where he will gestate for a night (or sometimes longer) and emerge reborn. During that night, negative energies, associations, and old wounds are drawn out by the earth, and it is these which are really buried when he rises from his grave the next day and refills it with soil.

The burial ceremony can therefore represent many things (sometimes all at once), depending on what the teacher and initiate require of it: a blessing, a healing, a way to let go of the past, a celebration of life, the embrace of a new future, or a form of vision quest to bring greater focus and clarity to life. It is both an ending and a new beginning.

"In some ways, the burial is like the initiation of the dragon cave that you completed in Wales with Adam and me," said Cad, "but its purpose here is quite different.

"Firstly, we have been talking of pilgrimages and their meanings, one of which is to change ourselves by entering a new dimension, or state of being ... a parallel universe, as we have called it.

"In the accounts of pilgrims, there often appears a 'dark night of the soul'—a need to let go of who they have been and a time of uncertainty as they do so before they are reborn and begin their homeward journey to remember themselves again. The burial offered to you here is an immersion in physical darkness, with the objective of aiding your journey from dark to light so you can find peace and balance and reach your destination with a purer soul.

"Like a seed, you are planted, and from that seed a new flower will grow. And so, secondly, the burial is about generation—or regeneration, I should say—and it is something, therefore, that every healer—or gardener!—should undergo, so they know what it is to absorb the energy of our planet and the healing that plants can offer. Every plant and every seed has, of course, already taken that journey into the earth and from darkness to light, and so it contains great power that we can learn from. The most effective way for us to do so is to become plantlike ourselves.

"Thirdly, I have spoken of Dunne and his revelations about time. In order to become more than mortal, he tells us that we must put ourselves into places where our minds can sleep and our dreams find wings. The womb of the earth is such a place.

"I also told you that there are tunnels beneath the earth—dragon paths that connect us to different dimensions—and in your grave tonight, you may find that this is literally true. Perhaps you will enter such a tunnel and create a new reality. Lastly, therefore, this is also an exercise, or an experiment, in conjuration: to see if you have the makings of a Merlin, who can, through wizardry, give birth to new worlds.

"I am older than you, and my days of exploring tunnels are behind me now, but I envy you your adventure and what you may discover in the lands beneath ours."

With that, he handed me the spade, and I began to dig the grave that would be my resting place for the night, while Cad gathered wood for a fire and longer branches and ferns that would cover me under the soil.

The grave itself, according to the instructions Cad gave me, did not have to be six feet deep, as is standard church practice, but only half that, as long as it was sufficient to lie in and be fully covered. It did not need to be box-shaped either, since there was no coffin involved, but rather an outline of the body so the person buried would be embraced and held by the earth.

Even so, to dig even a shallow grave is not easy, and the process takes some hours. Inevitably, during this time, one's thoughts turn to matters of mortality.

What is life anyway, its nature and meaning? According to the English poet Shakespeare, it is no more than "a walking shadow ... a tale told by an idiot, full of sound and fury ... signifying nothing."

The Bible tells us that we have "three score years and ten"—seventy years of life in total. Of these, however, the first ten or twenty are spent finding our feet (literally and metaphorically) and coming to terms with the world, while the last are for dreaming of past glories and preparing our souls for the next great adventure awaiting us. So perhaps it is truer to say that we really have thirty or forty years for fully living, when we are at the peak of our power and can achieve our purpose—or not.

Thirty years. It seems so little, especially as Adam believed that most people wasted even these because they were unaware of their purpose and did not really know what they were here to do. As a consequence, he said, they led unfulfilling and unfulfilled lives, which might, indeed, amount to no more than "sound and fury."

He had spoken to me once about the four orders of men, who, in his philosophy, made up the categories of the human race and described every person alive. They were the True Priests and Healers, the Fortunate, the Damned, and the Fools. Only the first group truly knew their reasons for being and lived them fully and passionately.

The Order of Fools, meanwhile, never understood their purpose. "They bumble through life not knowing what they're doing from one moment to the next," he had said. "Seekers without purpose, bees without hives, flowers without sunlight. Whatever they randomly create they also destroy at random, and then re-create it again, endlessly, over and over, because they have no clear direction in life."

The majority of us fell into the categories of the Fortunate or Damned and led unremarkable lives where, through luck or design, we became sinners or saints largely as a result of our unconscious actions, and it was only in the moments before death that we ever really understood our time on Earth, and then—with elation or, more often, regret—we saw the gifts we had been given and the things we had chosen to do with them.

At university, I had come across the work of Søren Kierkegaard, a philosopher who believed something similar. "Life can only be understood backwards," he said; the tragedy is that "it must be *lived* forwards."

We have so little time and such burning desires to accomplish something ... anything ... in the face of our annihilation. The knowledge that we are fleeting on the earth, like the shadows of clouds on a sunny day, is at times successfully, at others not so successfully, hidden from ourselves— and so we rush our lives or build dramas and monuments from them to achieve a sense of ever having lived.

> *Man that is born of woman hath but a short*
> *time to live, and is full of miseries.*
> *He cometh up and is cut down like a flower.*
> *He fleeth as it were a shadow,*
> *and never continueth in his stay.*
> *In the midst of life we are in death.*
> *Of whom may we seek succour but of thee, O Lord,*
> *Who, for our sins, art justly displeased.* [7]

How, then, should we comport ourselves in life? That is another question that has concerned the great philosophers.

"What is most important in this world?" Adam once asked. "Only love. We came here to explore, to adventure, and to play, but, in the end, only love is real, and that is where we should make our efforts.

---

7   From the *Book of Common Prayer*, "The Order for the Burial of the Dead."

"We must slow down to the pace of nature, not rush at life, and take our lessons from its gentle acceptances and the compromises it makes to accommodate its fellows. Then we, too, can come to know our passions and follow them with purpose, seizing every opportunity life gives us to turn chance into destiny.

"Whether an experience is good or bad is irrelevant, because they are only words—definitions delivered in our terms, based on our lives so far as we have lived them, and limited as we are in the knowledge of God or ourselves, which is much the same thing, really.

"We should never deny ourselves an experience, because every event we are privileged to be part of is an act of grace and a chance for us to learn and grow. Whenever we reject something or someone without consciously choosing to do so, therefore—because we are led by habit or prejudice, per-haps—we are really rejecting our lives. And it may also be that the very thing we said no to is, in the end, the one that would have given us more of the fat of life when we look back on our days and weigh our actions in the balance.

"The answer to life's mystery is, on one level, then, exquisitely simple: do more of ... whatever there is to be done! Commit to living as a Total Act, and allow yourself new experiences and opportunities whenever you possibly can!"

Did a night in a grave constitute a new opportunity for growth, I wondered, or to experience 'the fat of life'? I supposed that to Adam it would.

I climbed into my grave late in the evening. Cad offered a prayer for me and sprinkled salt—the traditional tool of purification used by sin eaters—beneath and around me, then covered the space above me with branches and ferns. It created a loosely woven structure to hold the soil he then piled over me. A small breathing space was left near my head so I would get air during the night. It took him a few minutes to arrange all of this, then he stepped away to sit by the fire. With that, the silent darkness descended.

It was more comfortable—and warmer—than I had thought it would be to lie within the soil. The earth held me closely, as if cradling me, but it wasn't claustrophobic, as I had imagined it might be, and I could shift my position if I needed.

The main difficulty, despite the quiet and the dark, was sleeping, because my mind was still so busy with the thoughts and questions of the day and the things that Cad had spoken of. But then, I imagined, the point of a burial like this was not to fall into a normal sleep but to ask those questions so that the soul of the world could answer. And so began a dialog with the "first mother," as Cad had referred to the earth, about life, purpose, meaning, the tunnels made by dragons, and all of the things I had learned that day.

After what seemed like hours, I began to notice light around me, which at first I took to be dawn. No birds sang, however, which was unusual, as their chorus is normally the first sign of the coming of day.

More unusual still, the light began to intensify, and I realized that it was not coming from outside at all but from inside the grave. It grew brighter until it engulfed me in white tinged with pale shades of green, blue, and mauve.

This luminosity did not just occupy my small enclosure either but streamed into the spaces above and below me, as if a new brilliance had taken over the world and I was no longer lying in a grave but a tube of light ... or a tunnel.

I reached up to the branches just inches above my head and, with a push, rolled them back like they were a carpet of fabric rather than a weave of plants and soil.

I stood up and found that the world was white, its natural colors bleached by the light that was now all around me. There was a noise, too, like a high-pitched hum, which drowned out other sounds.

I saw Cad sitting by the fire he had made and called to him, but he couldn't hear me above the noise (I could barely hear my own voice) and continued to stare into the flames, seemingly unaware of my presence. I was about to walk over to him to ask about the light, the sound, and the strangeness of it all, when, out of the corner of my eye, something moved.

At the very edge of the forest we were camped by, silent, still, and looking directly at me, was a small deer—a doe, really, since it was obviously female. It and the trees behind it were the only things not flooded by light.

It held my gaze for some minutes and then did something odd: it flicked its head as if calling me over, then turned and walked slowly into the trees.

I followed its summons and went towards it, then across the threshold of trees, into the forest with its blessed shade and shadows, closing my eyes for a moment and holding my breath as I readjusted to the normal colors and sounds of the world and the peace now around me. When I opened them again, I expected to see the doe, but she had vanished, and in her place there was a woman.

She had blond hair, just above shoulder length, turquoise-blue eyes, and the most perfect mouth, shaped like a bow, with pale pink lips. Barefoot and with no adornments, jewelry, or markings, she was dressed simply in a roughly fashioned dress of what looked like deerskin.

"My name is Melissa," she said. "Would you follow me if I had something to show you?"

Her phrasing was curious. It was not a command or even an invitation but a question: *would* you follow me *if* I had something to show you? But before I could say anything in response, she flicked her head as the deer had done and began walking deeper into the forest. Her question remained unanswered, and I followed her anyway.

Melissa. In Greek mythology, she was one of the nymphs who helped raise the infant Zeus and protect him from his father, Cronus, who had swallowed all of his other children alive immediately after their births. Hiding the child Zeus in a hill cave, Melissa fed him honey and the milk of the goddess Amalthea to help him grow strong so he could one day overthrow his father and become king of the gods, the "cloud-gatherer" himself.

When Cronus discovered Melissa's betrayal, he turned her into a worm, and not all the powers of Zeus could save her. The best the new god could do was transform her again, this time into a bee, one of the lowliest of creatures but a winged serpent or dragon, at least.[8]

"We are here," she said. She was standing in front of a tree like none I had ever seen: part oak, part hawthorn. Long spines grew from it, and into its shining black trunk was carved a familiar symbol: the *8* and the *B*.

"A friend of yours passed this way," she said simply. "He asked that, should you arrive here too one day, I present you with a gift."

With that, she snapped one of the long thorns from the tree and drove it into the flesh above my heart, dragging it downwards to lacerate the skin. At the same time, she kissed me with her perfect mouth, and I felt no pain.

"This is a guard," she said, rubbing herbs into the cut she had made, "a shield of protection offered by the plants. It will keep you safe no matter what life brings you.

"It is a mixture of herbs, among them chicory, rue, garlic, marshmallow, and fennel. It will repel bad spirits and make you immune to the actions of those who wish you harm.

"This is different," she continued, taking the thorn again and this time carving a deep half-moon into the skin

---

8   Bees are often regarded in folklore and mythology as "winged ser-
     pents" because of the venom carried in their stings, which gave
     them a snake- or dragonlike quality.

of my forehead. Immediately, my eyes began to water and blood from the wound poured into them, but she kissed me again and took away the pain once more.

Her artistry complete, she lifted the flap of skin she had made and scraped the flesh from beneath it, finally driving the thorn through the bone like a needle. "This is for clear sight and wise direction," she said, and began rubbing new herbs into the hole the needle had left: "Juniper, mugwort, pepper, and Good Saint John."

Her work done, she folded the skin back over my brow and looked into my eyes. "You were brave," she said, almost quizzically, as if it was a puzzle to her that I had not cried out. Then she offered me another kiss and, at the same time, slipped the deerskin from her shoulders. Her dress fell to the floor, and we embraced, becoming snakelike among the roots of the strange black tree.

I awoke some time later, and she was gone. Only a few deer tracks remained to suggest that anyone or anything besides myself had ever been there.

I made my way back to the grave and fell asleep once again inside it, but this time it was different: the sleep of the innocent and blessed; deep and luxurious, as if all cares had been lifted and all questions answered.

I only stirred when I tasted dirt in my mouth, then felt it raining onto my face. I looked up to see Cad stripping the ferns and branches from the hole above me. It was dawn, and the birds were singing.

"I trust you slept well," he said. "I thought I sensed you abroad in the field last night, but it can't have been you, of course, because, well, here you are, safely in the arms of the earth."

I didn't have the same confidence about what could or could not have happened during the night. The only thing I was sure of was that I had awoken famished and desperate for something to eat.

Sometimes miracles and visions must take second place to human needs and empty stomachs, after all. I had eaten little the day before and was pleased to see breakfast cooking on the fire.

5

The Nature of God and the Sun

Melancholy star!

Whose tearful beam glows tremulously far,

That show'st the darkness thou canst not dispel ...

Lord Byron,
"Sun of the Sleepless"

$\mathfrak{D}$AD HANDED ME a cup of herbal tea with a few bright leaves floating on its surface. "Lemon balm," he said. "It will relax you and take care of any aches the night may have brought. I added a little honey too."

I smiled inwardly. Lemon balm—what else would it be? A tallish plant, growing to about four feet, its leaves have a beautifully refreshing scent somewhere between lemon and mint, and at the end of summer it produces small white flowers that are full of sweet nectar. These botanical facts were not what amused me, however, but rather its genus name: *Melissa*, after the Greek for "honey bee"—the tiny flying dragons that are drawn to its flowers and aroma.

I had long ago stopped being surprised at "coincidences" like these because they seemed to arise so frequently in the presence of sin eaters and shamans. Years before, Adam had set me a dreaming task in which I was to find a plant ally, an essence or spirit of nature that I could turn to for guidance and counsel. In my dreams, I had met a female spirit who said that her name was Rachel and who had given me a rose as an ally. Minutes later, I woke up and went into Adam's cottage to find a woman there, whom he introduced to me as Rachel Rose. After that, nothing shocked me anymore.

I sipped the tea Cad had given me and ate the bread and honey he prepared while the fire took the chill from my bones. The sun helped too. It was rising now, and it looked like the day would be fine.

"Is there anything you wish to say about the events of the night?" he finally asked.

I had resolved the day before to be more open with him, and so, over the next several minutes, I went fully into my experience, telling him about the light that had flooded my grave like a new sun and that seemed in some way to expand it, creating a tunnel below my feet and above me instead of a hole with walls of soil. I told him about my encounter with the deer as well, and, holding up my cup to emphasize the point, of meeting the woman, Melissa. Cad sat silently, nodding occasionally, and listened. Finally, I told him about the strange tree, the mark of Adam upon it, and the herbs that Melissa had used on me.

"You received a lot of information," he said when I had finished. "It is interesting that you describe the light as 'a new sun.' Many travelers beneath the earth have also returned to talk of such a sun, though I have never seen it myself. I imagine I have not gone deep enough."

While I doubt now that this is exactly what Cad meant, it is true that there is a long history of scientific and other writing proposing what has come to be called the theory of a hollow Earth, with tunnels that run beneath it and a second sun that illuminates its core.

In 1692, Edmund Halley (after whom the famous comet is named) suggested in a scientific paper that the Earth we know might, in fact, be only a shell (800 km thick, to be precise), which contains inner spheres inhabited by other life. Leonhard Euler proposed a similar theory of an Earth with a small sun at its hidden center, 1,000 km across, providing light for civilizations at the middle of the world.

Science has suggested quirky ideas before, and neither of these proposals is therefore remarkable in itself—except for the tales of lost travelers who claim to have entered this inner world and met its inhabitants. One such account is given by Marshall Gardner in his 1920 book *A Journey to the Earth's Interior*, in which he included a diagram of the hollow world with an entrance at the North Pole.

But even this might not trouble our imaginations too much were it not for the strange case of Admiral Richard Byrd who, in 1926, became the first person to successfully fly over the North Pole. In 1929, he repeated his journey, this time over the South Pole, an expedition which did not go so well. During it, it is claimed, he went off-course, making a detour of 4,000 miles—into Earth's interior.

Perhaps there really are other worlds beneath us, lit by another sun and inhabited by beings who are like and unlike us, similar but radically different. That, however, is conjecture for another day.

"The herbs the woman used on you are also interesting," Cad continued, directing me back to a world more knowable.

"Those she placed in your heart have been used for magic and healing since at least the Middle Ages. Pliny wrote of chicory that people who anoint themselves with it 'become more popular and obtain their requests more easily.' Of rue, he said that the person who carried it would never be bitten by venomous creatures—whether snakes and reptiles or people who emulate their behavior. 'When about to fight with serpents,' he wrote, 'eat rue.'

"Garlic, as you know, is still regarded as one of our finest protections against plague, witchcraft, vampires, and scorpions, and increases courage and resolve. Marshmallow will keep the poisons of bees and snakes at bay, while fennel is a guardian of visions and sight.

"Of the herbs she rubbed into your dreaming and visionary center, here," he said, tapping my forehead lightly, "juniper has been used by sorcerers since medieval times to prevent fairies from spiriting infants away and to repel bad energies. Today we might say that its principal action is to safeguard us from becoming lost in the world and unable to find our purposeful ways.

"Mugwort was also used to protect travelers, and if wrapped around them, it would keep them safe from wild beasts and fatigue. Pepper carried by a soldier ensured his safety on the battlefield and brought him home unharmed, so it has a similar purpose.

"Good Saint John—St. John's wort—is, of course, a favorite of the Celts, and to us it represents the sun and its life-giving properties of health and happiness, direction, and growth.

"All of these are good omens for your journey, then, and more significant still since they were given to you by a 'bee woman'—the embodiment of a dragon—and beneath Adam's sign. I think we can conclude, therefore, that your old friend has conferred on you his blessing."

We sat quietly for a few minutes as I digested the information Cad had given me and his interpretation of events. I thought, too, about the herbal gifts that Adam had, through Melissa, imparted, and it occurred to me that, with

Cad here, I had a perfect opportunity to learn more about Adam and his friendship with Cad.

"How long had you known him?" I asked—aware as soon as I said it that I had used the past tense: *had*, as if he was gone forever. I corrected myself and rephrased the question. "What was he like when he was younger?"

"It is difficult to find a single word," said Cad, after a moment's reflection. "But if I had to, I suppose it would be stubborn. Bloody-minded might be even better."

I almost dropped my tea. I had only known Adam when he was older, not as a young man, but I had spent years in his company, and *stubborn* was not a word I would have used to describe him. *Irreverent, intelligent,* and *amusing* might be terms I would have chosen, but never *stubborn* or *bloody-minded*. Yet Cad knew him better than I did, and those were his words. I was intrigued.

"Men change over time," he continued, "but there are themes that run through all of our lives, and I would say that an unwillingness to conform in thought or deed was a theme of Adam's. When he was a young man, of course, he was also angry—as most young men are.

"His biggest failing—if it is a failing—is that he had no time for fools or people who had not thought through their positions but repeated the words of others, especially when they concerned what Adam considered the most important of all subjects: the soul and our provisions for it. His biggest issue was with the church.

"He had, you see, come from quite a religious background—but what I would call an *intelligent* religious background rather than one peopled by some of faith's blind followers, like we so often see today. His father read the Bible to him from an early age, but even though he was a simple man, his father understood the difference between a fable, a metaphor, a literal truth, and a lie in a way that even many priests did not, do not, or refuse yet to do.

"The Bible, you see—and as you may well know—is a collection of stories written by men, not God, and unlike gods, men are fallible, have their own agendas, and are filled with their own pomposity.

"As a book, the Bible is full of contradictions—as well it might be, since it was created over hundreds of years by many different authors as part of its colorful past. As a consequence, if you read it cover to cover, you will find it plotless and confused and lacking in both inspiration and guidance. God alone knows why it has been a bestseller for so many years—although *which* god is itself a mystery.

"It purports, for example, to tell the story of Jesus's birth—a story we are all familiar with. Mary, a magically pregnant virgin, gives birth to a son in a stable (or, in other versions, a cave) on December 25, an event that is announced by a star in the east and witnessed by three wise men. The ruler of the times, Herod, tries to have the baby killed, but he lives and is baptized by John, the good saint who is later beheaded.

"Jesus grows up to be a special man with supernatural powers: he walks on water, casts out demons, heals the sick, restores sight to the blind, and stills the sea with his power. He raises Lazarus from the dead and resurrects himself in Bethany.

"He has twelve disciples and comes to be known as the Lamb of God: the Good Shepherd carrying a lamb on his shoulders. All of this we know.

"What is less well known is that Jesus was not the only—or even the first—son of God. There was another who preceded him by a thousand years. This first son of God was Horus. He was conceived by supernatural means as well and born to Meri, the virgin who gave birth to him in a cave on December 25, a labor announced by the star Sirius and witnessed by three solar deities. The ruler of the times, Herut, also tried to have him killed, but he lived and was later baptized by Anup, who was subsequently beheaded.

"Horus had powers, too, that sound strangely like those of Jesus: he could walk on water, cast out demons, heal the sick, restore sight to the blind, and calm the sea. He raised Asar from the dead[9] and later resurrected himself in the city of Anu.[10] He had twelve disciples and was known as the Lamb, depicted with a shepherd's crook on his shoulders.

"Now, the thing about Horus is that he was not really the 'son of God' at all but the god of the sun. His birthday, December 25, is the first day after the winter solstice that is measurably longer. Hence the Bible, with all its twists and turns, misses the very point. It is the *sun*—not any one person—that is the Light of the World, and through it we gain life, growth, warmth, and all of the things we need for our survival. The sun, then, is the very emblem of nature, and this is our One True God.

---

9   Asar, as a mark of respect, was often referred to as "The Asar." In Hebrew, this is El-Asar. The Romans added the suffix *-us* to indicate a male name, resulting in El-Asar-us, or Elasarus. Over time, the E was dropped and the S became Z; hence, El-Asar became Lazarus.

10 Hebrews added the prefix *beth* (meaning "house") to the name Anu to produce Beth-Anu ("the house of Anu") as a description of a place and a lineage. Y and U were interchangeable in those days, and so Bethanu became Bethany.

"I might add that the Bible misses the point deliberately—mainly for political reasons and largely as a result of one man's actions: Constantine.

"Caesar Constantine, a lifelong believer in the powers of nature, had the misfortune to take over the Roman Empire in AD 306. Christianity was on the rise, although its doctrine was muddled and confused. Still, it had the attention of a powerful few who rejected the old ways and favoured the idea of a new, more distant god.

"I don't think Constantine was too concerned about that, however. What worried him more as a politician was the violence, disorder, and open conflict between Christians and believers in spirit. And so, in the summer of 325, he invited bishops from across the empire to the town of Nicea to decide on a common new religion. It was the first worldwide gathering of the church, and it was here that modern Christianity was invented.

"Among other things, the bishops took a vote on the nature of Jesus—if you can believe such a thing! One group thought Jesus to be divine and immortal, another that he was a remarkable healer but just a man, not divine at all, and this is what they voted on. The divine side won, and with that single political maneuver, the good bishops removed all power from nature and from ordinary people to determine their fates and take responsibility for their own lives, because Jesus the man could now no longer provide an example or an inspiration for people to aspire to. In the blink of an eye, all he had once represented was devoured instead by a god who could never be known.

"The good bishops cooked up a few other things at that meeting, too, including which gospels would go into the Bible. Then, as a final point of business, they ordered the burning of several books that they deemed heretical because they didn't support the vote they'd just taken and that, therefore—we can only assume—had a more sensible slant to them.

"Now, I would not want to suggest that Adam knew much about this as a young man. The truth of religion— that it is wholly invented—is, after all, still hidden knowledge to most people, and unlike me, Adam was never really a scholar. But he had an intuitive understanding all the same, and I have seen him storm out of churches muttering curses under his breath at what he regarded as the hypocrisy of preachers!

"One infamous occasion—which almost got him banned from the town—was when a preacher came to the church to lecture us about sobriety. Adam—and many others present—knew that the man himself was a drunk, but unlike the sheep in that preacher's flock, Adam would not just sit there and listen. He got to his feet and left.

"'He will be answering to God as well one day,' he said later, 'and if his God, by some horrible accident of fate, turns out to be the true God—one who condones lies and the condemnation of others—I want no part of Him and will take my chances with the other fellow!'

"He could be very outspoken at times and, as I said, bloody-minded. But he had a point. If the preacher had turned up and, from a place of honesty and personal experience, talked about 'the demon of drink,' I imagine that Adam would have been the first to applaud and give comfort. But he chose to address his problems instead by railing against others, which is a common and unfortunate solution that many choose in the face of their own illness.

"I think Adam would have liked to have been a fighter, actually, for a cause he truly believed in. But he was too young for the first war, too old for the second, [11] and by the end of those two great conflicts he had, I think, come to the conclusion anyway that all wars are abhorrent and entered into by dictators, no matter what their political colors. It was

---

11 At the beginning of the First World War (1914–1918), Adam would have been about thirteen; at the outbreak of the Second World War (1939–1945), he would already have been in his late thirties.

when he was in his twenties that things began to change for Adam and he started to find peace with himself. It was then that chance and destiny brought us a stranger."

The word *stranger* reminded me of something I had read in Adam's journal: "I remember the words of a stranger from long ago," he had written, "that we are food for the moon unless we lead a life of purpose."

"Who was he?" I asked.

Cad shook his head. "It is too long ago now for me to remember his name," he said, "or perhaps I never knew it. We spent only a fleeting time together, but I recall much of what he said because it was familiar to us from the traditions we already knew. If you wish, I can share it with you."

I nodded, and Cad began to speak.

6

The Stranger and the Purpose of the Moon

Strange are the ways of men,
And strange the ways of God!...
The portents of the sky,
The things that were of old.

Robert Louis Stevenson,
"Strange Are the Ways of Men"

𝕬s Cad related it, the stranger who had such an influence on them was in his fifties when they met him. A teacher, foreign to Britain, he was visiting Wales following a tour of Europe where he had been explaining his ideas to others. Evidently, he was a man of importance, but it wasn't this that attracted the young Cad and Adam, it was his philosophy.

Adam was especially fascinated, said Cad, because the stranger's thoughts so closely resembled his own and because they were such an antidote to the rhetoric that he had grown weary of. The stranger's interpretation of the Bible was quite at odds with that of the preachers, for example. He believed that there are passages in it which, if chosen and read with care, have important messages for us. They were not, though, the messages the church was promoting.

"The gospel of Luke tells us, for example, that the kingdom of God is to be found within us," said Cad, "not in buildings owned by the church.[12] This was liberating for Adam, because it meant that the power of nature was still intact and men could still determine their own fates.

12 Luke 17:21: "Behold, the kingdom of God is within you."

"The stranger taught that we must all wake up to this truth and make peace with it, because only then can we know our purpose—all of which was very easy for Adam to understand because he had his own views on this, which he called the Path of Purpose.[13] And so, to Adam, it was as if the stranger and he had found each other through some curious working of fate.

"The stranger said that human beings are not born with souls but must earn them by their actions. It was another point on which he and Adam agreed, for the Path of Purpose is the way to create a soul. Our souls may be immortal, that is, but the amount of soul we have—its depth and its quality—depends on how we have lived. And we cannot begin to live at all until we wake up to our lives and find our place within them.

"During his time with us, the stranger showed us some of the practices for soul-building that he had found and taught to others. One had to do with balance. Bringing the soul back to balance and returning it to its natural order (a process Adam called *at-one-ment*) is the aim of sin eating too, but we also learned that external balance is just as

---

13 This is explained in *The Sin Eater's Last Confessions*.

important because our actions in the world are so closely tied to the health of our souls.

"To develop our balance, we therefore began a sort of physical work where we would run full-pelt through forests, wade rivers, climb trees ... aware that at any moment one of us could yell *stop* and immediately then we would have to end what we were doing and hold ourselves in perfect pitch, even if we were clinging to the high branches of a tree or perching on a rock above a waterfall.

"As we caught our breaths, we observed the state of our bodies, emotions, and thoughts, and the extent of our connection to nature and spirit. The idea then was to track our feelings back to where they arose.

"Suppose I was afraid because of the position I found myself in—on the edge of a fall from a mountain, for example. Where exactly does that fear arise? Even death is just a process, after all, and a natural state of the world. All children know this and therefore lack fear, so they will take on any challenge. It is only as adults that we begin in our ways to cower in the face of our beliefs, and most often this is because we are afraid of losing touch with, or command over, what is familiar to us, and this is what we then teach our children. They are the vessels for our terrors.

"If we do not consider and prepare for our deaths, however—which are, in any case, inevitable—we do not consider our lives either, or our souls and how to perfect them. Instead, we imagine in our fantasies that we will simply go on forever, and at the same time we pass on our fears to others—our children and the generations who will follow them—so they can carry our burdens for us, and the world remains bound by terror.

"And so eventually the question must arise: who has taught us to be afraid—of falling, failing, dying, or making errors of judgment and asses of ourselves? And what are we prepared to do about that so we may liberate ourselves from someone else's fears?

"Having made our assessments, we brought ourselves back to balance by focusing on the purpose of our lives. Through this practice, we learned a great deal about ourselves and strengthened our resolve to become men of destiny.

"Another of the stranger's teachings concerned the need for efforts and challenges. Most people are opposed to both and will resist them at every turn, preferring the comforts and habits of a shallow life to the freedoms these challenges bring.

"There is something about making prolonged and sustained efforts, however, even when we are exhausted and believe we can't go on, by which we arrive at a place of awareness because we push ourselves beyond our normal boundaries and discover new dimensions to our beings. Through these efforts we enter parallel universes, if you will.

"The same is true when we step outside of ordinary circumstances and accept the challenge of new situations. Mystery surrounds and swells in us then, and, at least for a short time, we step outside of time and become more than the simple people we thought we were. You may have experienced something like this in the activities of yesterday: the physical effort of digging your grave ... the strangeness of the environment in which you spent the night ... or the realizations that came to you.

"Sleeping in our graves was a practice for Adam and me too, and what we learned—just as Mr. Dunne later described it—is that we are more powerful, eternal, and majestic than we have been led to believe. And once a man knows that, well, what is not possible for him?

"It is important that you understand, however, that the practices we embarked upon were not doctrines but experiments by which we could explore, through our own experiences, the depths and currents of our souls. The stranger was very clear that what he taught and what we discovered should not become a new gospel, for in the end, we all must murder our teachers ... not literally, of course," he added, looking up at me with mock suspicion.

"That we should murder our teachers is a turn of phrase, a way of saying that we must not fall back to sleep or, in laziness and lethargy, allow ourselves to follow others, because this is the curse of the world. The worst thing you can do is make a leader out of a teacher, because by virtue of this, they will always fail you—and then you will fail by association, and the world itself will turn sour.

"Our final practice together was a movement technique. Perhaps Adam showed it to you?"

I couldn't recall any movements I had learned from Adam apart from the walking meditation he had called moving at the pace of nature, so Cad offered to demonstrate the practice to me, and I joined him in it.

It looked and felt like tai chi, although it was unlike any of the forms I have subsequently studied. The moves were completed slowly in a continuous and gently flowing rhythm that began with us standing quite still and facing the sun, feeling its warmth as well as the breeze on our skin and, with eyes closed, listening to the sounds of nature with relaxed awareness to bring ourselves into balance.

Our arms were then extended to the sides at shoulder height and, with eyes now open, we twisted at the waist, turning left and then right, as if to look directly behind us.

"This circle we make is the sphere of our influence," said Cad. "Within it is contained all of the energy we have. Or, if you prefer, it is the extent of our souls. We are energy beings, you see; bigger than just our physical bodies but not so big that we own the world. At our fingertips, our energy merges with that of others so we are never quite separate from anything or anyone else around us. We blend and flow as our atoms become air, the carrier of information from spirit. Through an act of visualization, or 'true seeing,' and tuning in to the environment around us," he continued, "it is possible to draw in power and awareness from the air itself, as if our fingers were antennae receiving the wisdom of life."

The next movement was to bend the knees, keeping the back straight, and extend the fingers downwards until they touched the ground beneath us, so we absorbed the power of the earth in the same way as the air. Then, standing upright again, the arms were raised above the head to allow the energy of the earth to cascade over us and to receive the power of the sun.

Finally, the arms were brought to the sides, and the body came back to its first position. The movement ended with an affirmation, spoken aloud, which was Adam's addition to the stranger's process: "I am that which I am."

The words were not wholly Adam's, of course, but those spoken by God to Moses when the prophet dared ask his name. It must have amused the "angry young man" Cad had described to use these words in a new context like this, which was designed for achieving power instead of giving it away to a "make-believe god."

At the same time, in Adam's philosophy we are part of a god-energy which is, and forever will be, the knowing universe. His affirmation may have been a defiance of religion, therefore, but it was also a union with what is truly divine and a reminder of our strengths and responsibilities: "I am that, not another, and I take ownership of myself and my behaviors while also recognizing that I have no claims over anyone else."

Cad and I sat down again after completing our movements and sat quietly for a while as we watched the fire start to burn itself out. I felt relaxed and in tune with the world.

I was still intrigued by another comment in Adam's journal, however—something the stranger had apparently said: that without purpose, we are "food for the moon."

"Yes," said Cad. "That obviously caught Adam's attention too. In our tradition, you see, the moon is the first sin eater. Beneath it, the mournful dead—those who have not made their peace with the world and cling to it in need or remorse—wander the earth at night, and the moon feeds from their shadows.

"These souls are often not just lost but looking for endings: a way to say goodbye or to express their grief or remorse for some sin they have left behind them. Their business with the world is unfinished, and their mistakes still weigh on their souls. The stranger had seen this too. The moon feeds on humanity, he said.

"I think it is a gentle process, this feeding of the moon— a way for lost souls to free themselves from the embrace of the earth and become moonlight and stars and night clouds instead. But it is not ideal, nor can the spirits who are called by the moon find rest or return to us as allies and guides until the process is over. And so the job of the sin eater, as you know, is to free the sorrowful dead or ensure that their souls are never lost at all—because without this, the moon will surely take them."

"What do these lost souls want? What keeps them attached like this to the earth?" I asked.

"As well as the endings they seek, most often they want something that we simply cannot give them," said Cad: "our lives. If you allow me, we will take a short drive, and I will show you."

JUST OUTSIDE THE town of Bath there is a long barrow, thirty meters in length and thirteen meters wide, which has been a burial place since Neolithic times, some 5,000 years ago. It has remained an important ritual site for local communities until recently, and human bones were recovered from its chambers as late as 1816. Cad and I arrived there in the afternoon and took our place among the tourists who had come to absorb its mystery and admire its architecture, which had survived the elements for so long.

Unlike the others present, however, our intention was not just to admire but to explore certain truths about life and death that Cad wanted me to see. "The dead have much to say to the living," he said, "and the advice they offer is unique and precious. Do you see them?"

I looked around and saw a few people who had stopped like us at the barrow, but nothing that seemed unusual, and I wondered who he was referring to.

"Shift your focus," he said, signalling that I should use the way of seeing with peripheral vision that Adam had showed me and referred to as spirit-vision. I did so, but again there seemed nothing strange in this scene.

Just as I thought that, however, from the corner of my eye I noticed a sort of mist rise up from the ground. As I turned to it, it began to form a column, then gradually, as I held my attention, it cohered and became, if not exactly human, then humanlike.

It was staring ahead at the horizon and making the motions of walking towards it, but in fact it did not move anywhere. It was like it was stuck to the small parcel of land it occupied, walking on the spot but oblivious to that. It moved with a determination to attain a goal that, it seemed to me, it would never reach, and I wondered what actually drove it.

Once I had seen this one form, a dam broke and other apparitions rose up from the land on all sides of us, like sheets of early morning mist. Some emulated the futile actions of the first, grasping for the dreams of others, so conditioned in life that in death their spirits followed the same hopeless trajectory; others were freer in their movements but still wandered aimlessly, chaotically, or in circles, eventually returning to the place they had left without making progress in any direction. Only a few had more freedom of movement to walk where they chose, but even they were unable to leave the site itself, or perhaps were not interested in doing so.

"Who are they? Why are they here?" I asked in a whisper.

"The souls of the dead: food for the moon," Cad answered. "Many of them have never really used their lives and so don't even know they have died, because they have no point of comparison between their two states. See how they repeat their habitual actions, walking in place and making endless circles, just as they did in life. These are the spirits of people who lived without purpose—and now they are the dead without purpose.

"Others, like that one"—he pointed to a nearby figure—"weep for wrongs done to them or wrongs they have committed, and it is this which holds them to the earth: a longing for revenge or atonement.

"There are others who have a sort of addiction to life, and they are the most dangerous. The strong human emotions—lust, anger, greed, envy, pride ... all of the so-called sins of the world, as well as love itself—are the ones they are bound by. Only by being human can they experience these feelings again, and so, in their craving, they will take the lives of others in order to feel again. You have heard of such things, I am sure: spirit possessions and the visitations of succubae, poltergeists, and the like.

"The first thing we must do is protect ourselves from them, because they are as aware of us as we are of them, and their desire will be to control us. To ensure that they don't, we must draw power from the earth and surround ourselves with its light."

Following Cad's instructions, I closed my eyes and visualized a taproot of energy spiralling down from my body and drilling into the earth, where it connected with the life force of the planet and the hidden sun within it. I drew its energy into me like sap and felt it vibrate around me as a shield.

When I opened my eyes again, it was to one of the undead standing directly in front of me, just a few feet away, so we were face to face, although it was now unable to move any closer. I had the sense that it was male but that was almost impossible to tell from its appearance. Its destroyed face, eaten away by time, was really just bone and petrified ligaments. What remained of its grey-brown skin hung in clumps or was stretched like ancient leather across its cheeks, connected to a mouth that it could not close.

It looked directly at me, eye to eye, but made no sound. And yet, despite its appearance, I sensed not violence or anger from it but fear, desperation, and pleading—an addict, as Cad had said, begging for the fix of a living soul to slake its thirst for a life not led.

When it realized that it could not get any closer to me, it turned and moved slowly away. I thought I heard it moan, a low, keening sound of lament and hopelessness, but that may just have been my imagination playing tricks with the wind in the trees. I felt no fear of it but pity for what a fellow human being had become.

"Is there anything we can do?" I whispered to Cad.

"'More things are wrought by prayer than this world dreams of,'" he replied.[14] "We can pray for their release."

Then he added, almost as an afterthought: "You do know how to pray, I take it? For this is the first skill of the sin eater, and 'prayer is more than an order of words, the conscious occupation of the praying mind, or the sound of the voice praying...'"[15]

---

14 The lines are from Alfred Lord Tennyson, "The Passing of Arthur."

15 These lines are from T. S. Eliot, "Little Gidding."

Effective prayer, according to Cad's instructions, was a way of forming a bridge across dimensions so that the world became infused with our intentions, and through that, its nature would change—like parallel universes meeting in a single time and space according to our will.

It began by directing energy outwards from the top of the head in a thread that wound its way into the heavens to connect with God, in whatever way this god makes sense to us. I saw it as the great cloud of awareness that Adam had many times spoken of and that I had once seen for myself in the adventures I had shared with him. Through this thread, my will entered the cloud and began to spark there like a new idea illuminating the conscious mists around it.

When this communion was established, the next step in prayer was to draw down the power of God along this same connective thread so it became a living energy to be held in the solar plexus—the seat of power in the body—and fed with intent until it felt like a dizzying vortex of intensely spinning energy. Into it I projected images of the outcome I desired: the souls of the restless dead delivered to a place of peace.

When I felt this image to be as clear and strong as possible, I drew it up along the thread, through my body and out through my crown, like a shooting star making its flight to God and in its wake taking the gathered-in souls that had surrounded us so they would find their way home.

As soon as our prayers ended, the field felt quieter and more natural, as if things had returned to their rightful order. Opening my eyes, however, I saw that, despite our efforts, a few of the dead remained, wandering as aimlessly and mournfully as ever.

Cad saw my look of disappointment. "The dead must want to find peace before they can be helped," he said. "Those that remain are so attached to the flesh that we cannot help them now. Perhaps in a thousand years, when their appetites have waned, they might be released, but we can do nothing more now." And so we turned away, leaving the dead to weep and the tourists to their appreciative smiles and photographs, oblivious to the shadows around them.

Back at our camp, we spoke little more about these events. After the ritual of the night before and our efforts at the barrow, we were both tired and settled down to early beds instead. Cad slept soundly in his tent, and I did not wake until dawn, although my dreams were rich.

I dreamed of a sun who was a god, a sin-eater moon and, in a field of sorrows, an angry young man who raged at the sky to take back the souls that remained there to a paradise in the clouds that they had been born from.

7

The Pilgrim's Way

❧ Truly I tell you:
  No one may enter the kingdom of God
  Without being born of water and the Spirit.

John 3:5

WE ROSE EARLY again next day. It is difficult not to in the countryside, because our bodies adapt so readily to the rhythms of nature, and the real world wakes up at dawn.

Cad was making breakfast: a porridge of oats and water with salt, which he had sweetened with honey and berries harvested from the hedgerows that morning. He handed me a mug of it, and I sat down next to him.

"This will be our last day together … on this journey, at least," he said. "I made a promise to Adam that, should you pass my way, there were things I would show and teach you, and I have done that. You now know that there are other universes made up of life choices and opportunities that are linked by the dragon paths we walk. You also know that there are some who deny themselves these choices and end up lost or controlled in life and equally lost in death. Some of them you met yesterday. In short, you know the greatest secret of our craft: that the mystery of life and death is resolved by the will. It is our *purpose* that matters.

"There is much more that you do not know, of course, but we don't have time for that now, and in any case, with what you *do* know, you also have the opportunity, should you wish to take it, to learn other truths for yourself. And so today we have one further order of business, and then I will step aside and leave you to your quest. This final business is a blessing for your journey."

He asked me to remove my shoes and socks as he brought out a basin filled with water and herbs. I had taken similar baths made by Adam. Usually they signified an event of importance and provided a means of cleansing the spirit as much as the body, so that we approached matters of the soul with a pure and proper attitude.

Adam had poured the waters over me and, expecting the same from Cad, I stood up in readiness, but he told me to sit down again and began to bathe my feet instead, using bunches of herbs in place of a cloth, which he squeezed to release their fragrant waters.

There was something quite moving about this simple ceremony, but it was also embarrassing to have someone older than me, whose wisdom I respected, humbling himself in this way. I would have preferred to have bathed myself, but then, I supposed, it would not be a blessing if it was not conferred by another.

Cad shared none of my concerns. "This ritual," he said, matter-of-factly, "is referred to in the Bible, in the story of

Jesus washing the feet of his disciples,[16] although it has a history that far predates Christianity. Thanks to the decisions taken at Nicea, however, its meaning has mostly been lost. It can be intuited, though, and its importance gleaned from the fact that even the good bishops of Nicea chose to keep this ritual among the writings and practices recorded in their new Bible. Its meaning is this: that there are herbs that contain the powers of the earth, and that by using them, we gain in strength and wisdom.

"Perhaps to us this does not seem so controversial, but for some it is still a very dangerous truth. It would not do, for example, for people to know how to take blessings for themselves from the earth, because this undermines the power of the church. And so it has become the practice of priests these days to bless the herbs themselves instead of the herbs blessing the people. The implication is that the church has a power greater than that of the earth or of the god who created it!

"The ritual of the priests is called the Blessing of Herbs on the Feast of the Assumption. It takes place each year on August 15, and it is interesting to us because it contains the vestiges of a much earlier knowledge: that herbs and bless-

---

16 John 13:1–35.

ings are connected, and that plants offer us divine protection for body and soul.

"The origin of the Christian practice is not without interest either. According to tradition, Saint Thomas and the Apostles made a pilgrimage to the tomb of the Virgin following her death but, on arrival, they discovered her body gone. Her resting place, instead, was filled with fragrant herbs and flowers. Faced with this mystery, the belief arose that Mary's body had been assumed into Heaven and the herbs left as a reminder of her divine essence. The Blessing of Herbs on the Feast of the Assumption should logically, therefore, be a way for Christians and others to receive blessings from the Virgin on this special day. Instead, for the reasons I mentioned, the church has reversed the ritual so that the priest now offers blessings to the plants of the earth. A little presumptuous, you might think.

"That is not the end of this story, however, because the bodiless tomb became an embarrassment to the church and its explanation of assumption a convenience for them to explain their loss. However, the idea appears first not immediately after Mary's disappearance but in a treatise written by Good Saint John some 400 years later.[17] It sounds very

---

17 *De Obitu S. Dominae.*

much like the good saint didn't really know what had happened either but was doing his best to tie up loose ends. The church grabbed his explanation with both hands. After all, it said, Jesus had announced at the Last Supper that he would go and prepare a place for his family and return for them so that 'where I am, you may be also'—and where he was, it had already been decreed at Nicea, was in Heaven.

"There is another possibility, though, and another interpretation of Jesus's words: that Mary did not die and was not assumed into Heaven but remained very much alive, and that Jesus really did go somewhere—on Earth, not in Heaven—to prepare a place for her and the rest of his family. I mention this now because there are some who believe that this 'somewhere' is the same place you are destined for: Glastonbury."

I was fascinated by this Christian mystery, but Cad had realized, I think, that he was straying from the matter at hand and brought his attention back to the ceremony.

"I will tell you more about this later," he said. "For now, you should know that the herbs in this bath are lavender, which Mary was fond of because of its virtues of protection and cleanliness; periwinkle, so the Devil will have no power over you; clary, the 'eyes of Christ'; and mint, which is still strewn in the aisles of churches for the Virgin's procession.

They are plants of protection, blessing, and for the reclamation of power."

Having explained the herbs, he continued washing my feet and also began quietly to pray:

"Our help is in that which made Heaven and Earth: all flesh shall come to you.

"You have given water to the earth and enriched it. Fill up this small stream, too, and multiply its powers to heal and deliver us." (Nodding towards me, as if I was the "small stream" to be filled.)

"You have created all things visible and invisible, including plants and trees and men, so that each should flower according to its season and nature, and so that plants should be our medicine in times of need.

"We pray that you bless these herbs and the powers that are in them so they protect us against tribulations, the poisons of serpents, and the bee-stings of snares and deceits. Grant us also that through their powers we may be received into the Holy Land in accordance with our merits and deeds. *Caritas.*"[18]

---

18 The words of this prayer seem to be adapted from the Catholic Blessing of Herbs on the Feast of the Assumption. For comparison, a more orthodox version, translated by the Most Reverend J. H. Schlarman, is available at www.catholic.org/prayers/ (accessed May 20, 2008).

He stood up when he had finished and turned away. I was about to stand too and put my shoes and socks back on, but he stopped me. "We are about forty miles from Glastonbury now," he said. "In our car, this will probably take us two hours! But I cannot transport you the whole way, I am afraid, since it is the duty of the pilgrim to walk at least some of the journey and to reach his destination barefoot. This is another reason for the ceremony we have performed: so the feet which enter the Holy Land begin their travels clean."

I thought of Adam and his penchant for going barefoot most of the time. "We are always on a pilgrimage," he had written in his journal. Perhaps that was why he so often went without shoes. I had also taken to going barefoot some of the time too, even on social occasions, which sometimes brought strange looks from the other people present who had forgotten, no doubt, that they came into this world barefoot and naked as well.[19] Still, the thought of walking the English roads without shoes for at least some of the remaining forty miles left me less than delighted.

---

19 In fact, going barefoot is very good for the body, as it stimulates the many hundreds of nerve endings and reflexology points in the feet. Wearing shoes, meanwhile, constrains the feet and can lead to physical problems.

"You can be grateful, then, that you are not attempting the pilgrimage to Santiago de Compostela, which is a distance of around 500 miles!" said Cad. "The most devout of its pilgrims walk the whole route barefoot or even crawl the entire way!"[20]

Hearing that, it was difficult to feel sorry for myself, and my spirits lifted again when Cad said he would take me by car to within five miles of Glastonbury anyway. Even barefooted, I was sure I could walk the remaining distance.

We used soil and the remaining herbal water to douse the fire, then packed up our things and spent a little time at the site to make sure that the land was returned to its former state, as if we had not been there at all.

"Not total invisibility," said Cad, looking over to the gravesite. It had been refilled with soil and the turf placed back on top of it, although the level of the grass would be

---

20 The route traditionally taken on this pilgrimage starts in St. Jean Pied de Port and finishes in Santiago de Compostela. It is possible to start or finish anywhere, however, and some continue on past Santiago to the sea at Finisterre, which was thought in medieval times to be the end of the world. The name Compostela comes from the Latin *campus stellae*—"field of stars"—and arises from the legend that the bones of Saint James were buried in a field near the town. Some time later, a shepherd was guided to the burial site by a star, and a church was built over the relics. This was later replaced by the Cathedral de Santiago de Compostela.

uneven until the land had a chance to settle, which nature would take care of in time.

Our work done, we threw our things into the car, and Cad started the engine. "There is a major dragon line between Wales and Glastonbury," he remarked after a while. "It is not just an energy line or a ley, but one based in faith and mystery: a true path of the heart," he said.

"The history of Glastonbury—*Ynys Witrin*, the Glassy Isle—can be traced to 4,000 years BC. That was the time of the first lake village: a man-made island built from hand-felled trees.

"Life was probably uneventful there, although it must have been hard to live among the elements in a land of water and forest where wild boar, bears, and wolves roamed free. In AD 63, however, things changed, and the mysteries of Avalon began. It was then that Joseph of Arimathea, the uncle of Jesus, arrived in Glastonbury.

"Joseph had made many journeys to England before to trade for tin with Cornish miners, and on one occasion it is said he brought his young nephew with him. Legend has it, in fact, that Jesus was, for a time, a miner at Priddy, a village just outside the town of Glastonbury.

"When Joseph returned in AD 63, however, he arrived with twelve travelers from Jerusalem. Pausing at Wearyall

Hill, he thrust his cane into the ground, and it took root there and began to flower. It does so still and is known as the Glastonbury thorn.

"It is interesting, therefore, that in your vision in the grave you saw a tree that was half-oak and half-thorn. The oak is a symbol of the Celts and the thorn a symbol of Glastonbury. We can take this as a further sign, therefore, that the Celt you are seeking has indeed passed this way.

"Joseph took the flowering of the thorn as a sign as well: that he should build a church in the land of Avalon. The king granted him a thousand acres so he could begin.[21] It was not a great ornate temple in some crucifix form, however, like the churches of today. The first Christian building in Britain was, in fact, a circular hut made simply of wood and wattles ... everything natural ... and everything in nature wants to be a circle.

"It is fascinating to speculate who Joseph's traveling companions might have been, don't you think—or, rather, who in particular might have been among them? Remember I told you that Mary's tomb was quite empty when Thomas

---

21 Aviragus was the king of this region at the time and actually gave Joseph 12 hides, or 1,440 acres of land. See, for example, *Glastonbury: Maker of Myths* by Frances Howard-Gordon (Gothic Image Publications; currently out of print).

found it, and that Jesus—who already knew Glastonbury—was also missing and presumed in Heaven. But perhaps there is a more practical and less esoteric explanation ..."

"The twelve travelers were the members of his family?" I interrupted.

"Well, why not?" said Cad. "They had been persecuted by the Romans and betrayed by their own people in Jerusalem, and Jesus's last words on the night before his crucifixion had been that he would go and prepare them a new place. Why wouldn't he have meant it literally: a place he knew and liked, which was far enough from his homeland to avoid persecution there? I would if I was in his position!

"Where our story becomes more fascinating, though—for a Welshman, at least—is around AD 560–580. It was then that Saint David—one of the spiritual founders of Wales and the town that Adam and I grew up in—had a dream that led him to Glastonbury.

"A dream may be a dragon path too, or at least herald its presence. David followed his, arriving in the town with the intention of consecrating the church that Joseph had built and which was now part of a much larger abbey.

"As he looked at it, however, the world shifted for David, and he had a vision that it had already been consecrated—by Jesus himself, in honor of his mother. And so, according to this legend, Jesus had indeed been present in Glastonbury—and, perhaps Mary too, which would again explain her disappearance.[22]

"But I wonder if there was not another reason for David's arrival in the town? Much later, in 1184, you see, there was a fire in the abbey's old church, on the site of the one built by Joseph, and during its restoration, the monks made a curious find: an old oak coffin buried sixteen feet beneath ground which contained the bones of a man and a woman. A stone slab had hidden the coffin and, when it was lifted, an inscription was found on its underside. *Hic iacet sepultus inclitus Rex Arturius in insula Avalonia*: 'Here lies buried the famous King Arthur in the Isle of Avalon.'

"Scholars believe that Arthur died somewhere around AD 540–560, and David arrived in Glastonbury close to this time. So perhaps his consecration of a church (which never took place) was not the real—or, at least, the only—

---

22 William of Malmesbury, a twelfth-century historian, writes in his *Gesta Regum Anglorum* ("Deeds of the English King") that David visited Glastonbury intending to dedicate the abbey and donate an altar to it, which included a large sapphire. Before he could do so, however, Jesus appeared to him and told him that "the church had been dedicated long ago by Himself in honor of His Mother, and it was not seemly that it should be re-dedicated by human hands." So David commissioned an extension to the abbey instead, which was built near the site of Joseph's original church.

reason for his being there. Perhaps he needed to keep an appointment with a dying king. For Arthur, it is believed, was also the guardian of a magical treasure: the Holy Grail.

"The Grail is thought by some to have been the chalice used at the Last Supper and to catch the blood of Jesus when he was speared on the cross—a relic brought to Glastonbury by Joseph.

"But what if it was not a literal chalice or the literal blood of Jesus that it contained, but his blood-*line*? What, in fact, if Jesus's family included a child he had conceived with another of the Marys in his life—his wife, the Magdalene—and it was *this* that Arthur and his knights had protected—knowledge that now passed to David?

"It would have to be kept secret, of course, because, after the pronouncements of Nicea, Jesus and God were one, neither of them flesh and blood but deities ... so what would Jesus be doing with a wife or fathering a mortal child?

"To protect the power of their new Christian doctrine, the rulers of the church could not have the truth of Jesus's humanity revealed, and his family would therefore have been at risk from the very people who had deified him, because, according to them, Jesus had already ascended to Heaven.

"I doubt that any of this will be proved, but it just may be that when you reach Glastonbury, you will be walking among the descendants of Jesus. Don't let it go to your head, though! Remember: he was a man, not a god, just like you and me."

It is an intriguing thought that there may have been a connection—some form of dragon path—between Joseph, the bloodline of Jesus—the *sang réal,* or "royal blood," of the Holy Grail—King Arthur, the Grail's defender, and Saint David; a connection which stretched from the Isle of Avalon to the villages of Wales and united the two Celtic nations and their saints, shamans, and sin eaters.

Certainly, the presence of all of these men in Glastonbury is established either in the history or among the many mysteries of the mist-shrouded isle, while the legends of Arthur remain rich and thick across the land.

With hindsight, however, I am not sure that Cad's theory can be entirely accurate. For one thing, Geoffrey of Monmouth gives the date of Arthur's death as AD 542 in his *Historia Regum Britanniae* (History of the Kings of Britain), and David may not have arrived in Glastonbury until AD 580, so there is a gap of some years to suggest that an audience with the dying king would not have been possible.

On the other hand, Geoffrey's is not an entirely accurate historical record, and he did allow himself a dramatic or novelistic approach to writing, so the date of Arthur's death may have been later than he claims. But even if he is accurate, the years between the death of Arthur and the arrival of David are not, in the span of history, so great that the secrets of the Grail could not have remained hidden by being passed to another guardian during this time.

To add to the mystery, the standard text on Saint David (the Welsh *Dewi Sant*) is *The Life of Saint David*, or *Buchedd Dewi*, written by the eleventh-century scholar Rhygyfarch. It was an eventful life, according to the writer, which began with the rape of his mother and his eventual birth in the midst of a violent storm.

Even in the womb, however, he was able to perform miracles. One story tells how his mother, during her pregnancy, visited a church to hear the sermon of the priest, but he was struck dumb in the presence of David and the radiance that emanated from the still unborn child-saint and the woman who carried him.

David went on to cure his teacher, Saint Paulinus, of blindness, and soon after this, he healed King Proprius of the same affliction. His fame as a spiritual healer thus grew and he became known as the Waterman because of his fondness for the ritual purification of the sick and sinners using herbs and water.

In later life, he made a pilgrimage of his own to Jerusalem and upon his return delivered the Synod of Llandewi Brefi (the place in Wales of Cad and Adam's birth), where he spoke so eloquently that a hill miraculously rose up beneath him so that his words would be carried throughout the country.

It is strange, then, that after this busy life of adventure and miracles, little is known or written about the saint following his return from Glastonbury. It appears that whatever he saw or discovered there, he held his silence about it until his death in AD 589. Some believe that he returned to Wales carrying the Grail with him.

Perhaps there is some truth to Cad's theories, then; perhaps not. Either way, the myths of Wales and of Glastonbury run deep.

8

The Well of the Grail

I arise from dreams of thee
And a spirit in my feet
Hath led me—who knows how?
To thy chamber-window, Sweet!

Percy Bysshe Shelley,
"Lines to an Indian Air"

We had been driving for an hour or so when Cad pulled the car over to the side of the road. "This is where I leave you," he said. "Before I do so, though, I have this final gift for you."

He pulled a small pouch from his pocket. "Pilgrims carry talismans," he said, "and this is yours. Hang it around your neck.

"It contains three items: rose petals, an ally which has some significance for you, I believe; the petals of daffodils, a symbol of Wales and the man you are seeking; and a candle from the church of Saint David. With these you have the power to create ritual, which is all we ever really need to help us when we are operating in the spiritual realms. Perhaps you will make a thanksgiving ceremony when you find your friend."

I thanked him and we shook hands, then I stepped out of the car. It was the briefest of farewells, even though we both knew that we might not see the other again.

Cad drove off in a vehicle that was even dirtier than when we had started, and for a moment I savored the silence of a country road, feeling that strange mixture of relief and aloneness when an intense time spent in another's company finally comes to an end. My life had been so entangled with Cad's in the last few days that it was nice to feel the space around me again. At the same time, for the first time in days, I was completely alone. I picked up my bag and started walking towards the town.

A mile or so further on, it occurred to me that I hadn't looked at Adam's journal for a while and I wondered if it might contain anything that would shed light on the subjects that Cad had been speaking of. I sat down on the grass alongside the road, pulled the journal from my bag, and flicked to a few pages at random.

◆ ◆ ◆

> *Still-lives are what most people live. They seek healing for their solitude most of all, but their wounds are often deeper than surface- or even soul-level, bound up as they are with a world and a way of life that denies them community, conscience, or a right to choice and responsibility.*
>
> *"The love of money is the root of all evil," the Bible tells us, but really it is a love of—or need for—power that drives us in a world where people are lonely and*

*live in fear. Love and connection is what their souls
crave, and they may even betray their friends—or
themselves—to feel loved. They give up their power in
return for affection.*

*Certainly we are confused, and neither our
technology nor our "genius" can heal us. Money
and power concern us, but those who chase these
phantoms seek more than they can offer.*

✦ ✦ ✦

I thought about a Jesus who may have arrived in Glastonbury sick of what was going on in his name. He had started
out in life as a simple carpenter and became a man of
power: a respected spiritual teacher and healer. As a result
of this, however, he had also become the accidental founder
of a religion he did not choose and which at the time of his
death or disappearance had already become a new "corpo-
rate Christendom" with a momentum all its own.

"Foxes have holes and birds of the air have nests, but
the Son of Man has no place to lay his head," he had com-
plained at the end of his Sermon on the Mount.[23] "Follow
me," he had asked of the crowd there: be like me, act in the

---

23 Matthew 8:20.

ways I act, but do not give your power to me or to others, or feel that you must become part of a movement where I am all that matters. "Let the dead bury their own dead."[24]

He sounds in some ways like a weary CEO, and I could understand how such circumstances might drive a man or his family into secret exile in a place they had known in simpler times and how their presence there would need to be guarded.

It was clear, too, that Arthur would have offered ongoing protection for this great secret if that was what had been asked of him by the descendants of Jesus. Arturus, the bear-man and warrior whose passion was for truth, not gain, would surely have offered himself as their gatekeeper.

♦ ♦ ♦

Original sin—our only sin—is to forget who we are and what we stand for. The world makes it easy for us to do so and to stray from the path. When life is random, its patterns only emerge when we imagine them as part of the world. It is not God who breaks the hearts of lovers, then, or kills the old, the children, or the spirit of the world through jealousy, pain,

---

24 Matthew 8:22.

*revenge, or the worship of what will ultimately prove
to be false. Nor is it chance or fate, but destiny: the
meanings we choose to impose.*

*And yet we are such a hopeful and brilliant people.
Anything that can be imagined is real—not only
possible, but, on a planet as big as ours, already
happening right now at least somewhere on Earth. All
we need is better dreams and the transformation of
these into visions and then action through the power
of our will.*

*But few will take this step, dependant as they are on a
world that has been dreamed for them by others. Our
greatest sorrow, then, is that, in our final hours, the
things that will cause us most regret are not the evils
done to us but those we did to ourselves and to others
because we lost our way. The failings of other people
are easy to forgive, but our betrayal of ourselves is
harder for us to find peace with.*

*I have heard that Australians take a walkabout
when they are young, to remember themselves and
reacquaint their souls with purpose. They remain in*

the wilderness, close to nature, alone and self-reliant for months, tracing the songlines their ancestors walked and honoring the deeds of their heroes. They leave their villages as children, but they return as adults who know the truths of the world.

We do not have an education like this, but we have our dragon paths, like the songlines of aboriginals, and we must walk them if we are to become men of purpose like them. If not, we remain children, dependant on others for our rewards, until finally we come to know the pang of regret.

> *What the dead had no speech for when living*
> *They can tell you, being dead.*
>
> T. S. Eliot, "Little Gidding"

The dead can teach us much—both our good ancestors and the heroes who have evolved beyond the web of lies, and those who have never really lived at all. The first we can learn from and emulate; the second we must refuse to be.

*All freedom begins with such a refusal to be caught
in the traps of the world. We must put our faith in
what sings to us and in the places where truth can
be found: nature, in all of the forms, signs, and the
omens it brings us. We must trust the sacred—but
never those who tell us to, because their ideas of
truth will usually come with their needs and a price
attached! Sin, salvation, and what is truly sacred;
these are matters for each human heart to discover so
that life becomes sweet.*

*The songlines, dragon paths, and pilgrimages we are
on, these are our lives, and we must keep faith with
them.*

◆ ◆ ◆

Adam's journal was painting a depressing picture, which
was unlike him, although I imagined that his reflections on
the human condition were, sadly, true, especially at the time
of my journey. In the 1980s, Britain seemed concerned only
with money, power, and status—not so very different, in
fact, from today. Adam's solution, as he had told me often,
was to act willfully with kindness and compassion in order
to break the conditioning of the world and escape the hold

of those who would, for their own sakes, have us submit to a belief in fear, separation, and the need for leaders and saviors.

"Each of us has the power to love willfully and with passion, so we cling fiercely to what is human and godlike within us instead of following the rules of others, which invite us to lose our selves and our souls," he had said. "We must stay true to love, and 'do the little things'—*Gwnewch y pethau bychain mewn bywyd*—as Saint David urged his followers, so we help one another each day and remind ourselves of the journey we share."

I closed the pages of his journal and was about to walk on when I heard a car, the first that had approached me on this road. It stopped a few feet in front of me: a yellow Volkswagen with daisy transfers and peace signs on the back—a typical Glastonbury hippie car. It reversed back a little, and the passenger door creaked open. The driver leaned across and looked out. "Would you like a lift?" she asked. "I'm going into town if you're heading that way."

Something about her eyes and her hair—blond and just above shoulder-length—seemed familiar to me. She was, I would say, in her early thirties; older than me, and it was this, I supposed—as well as the spiritual openness that

Glastonbury is known for—which gave her the confidence to stop and offer a ride to a stranger on a country road.

Barefoot, disheveled, and probably ten years younger than her, I imagine I looked like a hippie myself and hardly much of a threat to her anyway. Times were also different then: more innocent and trusting.

As she waited for my answer, she looked me over and added: "You look like a pilgrim of the dragon path."

"Pardon?" I asked, shocked that she would know anything about pilgrims and dragon paths or recognize such a pilgrim if she saw one. Perhaps it was something about Glastonbury or the sort of people who came there. Maybe it attracted pilgrims; although, from her comment, clearly not that many.

"I said: you look a bit grim there on the grass," she said, smiling. "I wondered if you needed some help."

"Oh," I said, "I thought you said something else."

I suppose I did look grim. I had been pondering Adam's solemn words as she had driven past. Despite his views about a world where people were lost and unhappy, Adam was more of an optimist than his journal would suggest, and he retained faith in human beings to correct the faults he saw in society as long as we made an effort to help each other in small ways as a gesture of love and support. Then, right on cue, as if he'd planned it as an example of what he had in mind, a car had stopped with an unconditional offer of help.

Despite this good omen, and as much as I would have liked a lift, I didn't feel that I could accept one from the smiling woman in the car because I had made an earlier commitment to Cad, and to Adam and myself, that I would walk into Glastonbury barefoot, following the pilgrim's way.

That was not something I wanted to tell her, though. I didn't feel comfortable describing myself as a pilgrim, with all that the word might imply, and she might in any case think me crazy if I did. So I thanked her for the offer but declined it, saying that I wanted to walk.

"OK then! No problem. Enjoy it! It's a lovely day," she said, pulling the passenger door shut again and driving slowly off.

The interaction spurred me on, however, and made me feel better about the possibilities of the world. I stood up and started walking, following her car for a little way down the road until it rounded a bend and was gone.

I reckoned I still had about three miles to go before I reached the town. A little way on and my feet began to feel hot from the friction of the road, so I tried to use the grass at the roadside when I could, although brambles, hidden stones, twigs, and old wood from the hedgerow made it just as painful in other ways, and I was snagged by briars, leaving scratches and sores. By the time I reached Glastonbury, my feet were in a sorry state altogether, blistered and bleeding in parts.

I entered the town by Wellhouse Lane, along which are the Chalice Gardens with their famous well, fed by the Red Spring that flows down from Chalice Hill, where Joseph is said to have once hidden the Holy Grail. The water it contains is blood red and believed to have healing properties. With that in mind, I walked into the gardens and sat down at the well-side to wash the dirt from my feet and tend to my cuts.

The well itself is protected by an oak and iron cover decorated with the ancient symbol of the vesica piscis—an elaborate figure eight: the sign that had started me on this quest when I first saw it in Adam's journal. I smiled when I saw it again here. Chance and destiny once more, symbolizing perhaps that my journey had indeed come to an end.

The vesica piscis is regarded as a shape with mystical properties, made by the intersection of two circles, both of the same radius, so that the center of each lies on the circumference of the other. Translated from the Latin, the name of this design means "bladder of the fish," the fish being another ancient symbol for the Christ. It has been used in religious seals for thousands of years. Here, it was also dissected by a sword: the magical Excalibur of King Arthur. Seeing this, my thoughts turned again to Cad's speculations about the true nature and destiny of the Grail.

Before I could get much further, however, someone else came into the gardens and, looking up, I saw that it was the woman who had offered me a lift earlier in the day. "Hello again," she said. "You made it! Welcome to Glastonbury!" Then, staring down at my feet and my attempts to soothe them, she added, "May I help you?"

It was a genuine question—*may I?*—rather than polite words offered while the help is actually given, as is often the case with a question of this kind, and she hung back and waited for my response. Only when I nodded did she kneel down next to me and begin pouring the water over my feet, gently massaging them as she did so. And so, for the second time that day, at the start and end of my walk, once by a man and once by a woman, both in the presence of a symbol, I was offered a blessing of water and the spirit.

As she worked on me, I remembered where I knew her from, or who she reminded me of, at least. *Melissa.* I had met her before in my burial dreams of a goddess of the forest who healed me with herbs and kisses.

Adam taught that when we look for omens, we should pay special attention to those that come in threes. This is what I had done in that field in Wales on the first day of this adventure and the signs that I received then—the cloud, the tree, and the gate—are what had brought me to this town. Now, again, I was receiving three signs: the deer-woman I had met in a dream, the woman on the road, and the one now kneeling before me offering healing, all of them the same woman.

"Your name wouldn't be Melissa, would it?" I asked casually.

She looked up. "Not quite," she answered. "It's Melanie, but most people call me Mel."

It was close enough. The name Melanie comes from Melaina, one of the three oracles and sisters of the healing springs of Delphi who interpreted the future and the signs and omens of nature. It means "black" or "dark," suggesting that Melaina presided over the hidden aspects of prophecy and the soul.

"There are three holy ones, sisters born—three virgins gifted with wings," says one of the Homeric Hymns. "From their home they fly now here, now there, feeding on honeycomb and bringing all things to pass. And when they are inspired through eating yellow honey, they are willing to speak the truth; but if they be deprived of the gods' sweet food, then they speak falsely, as they swarm in and out together."[25]

"They are in a word 'Melissae,'" writes the scholar Jane Harrison. "Honey-priestesses, inspired by a honey-intoxicant; they are bees, their heads white with pollen."[26]

The name Melanie also has a connection to Mella, the mother of Saint Manchan, an Irish monk who was sent in the seventh century to a remote island to build a monastery there and teach the word of God, much as Joseph had done when he arrived on the island of Glastonbury. Manchan built a monastic cell for his mother, which was joined to the monastery by a small bridge. Beneath it, according to the saint, there flowed:

> *A little pool but very clear*
> *To stand beside the place*

25 *Homeric Hymn IV: Hesiod, the Homeric Hymns and Homerica*, translated by Hugh G. Evelyn-White (BiblioBazaar, 2007).

26 Jane Ellen Harrison, *Prolegomena to the Study of Greek Religion* (Princeton University Press, 1991). The "honey-intoxicant" she writes about is fermented honey, or mead, a drink that Adam was fond of and often shared with me as a form of meddeglyn (or myddyglyn), the Welsh for "medicine."

Where all men's sins are washed away
By sanctifying grace [27]

Both of these origins or connections to Mel's name had therefore to do with water, healing, and divination—and here we were, in another time, place, or parallel world, meeting for the third time at the site of a holy well.

"Do you have anywhere to stay yet?" she asked, suddenly standing.

"No," I replied. "I've only just arrived."

"Then you must stay with me," she said. "I have a guest-house. The rooms are cheap and there is hardly anyone else there now, so you're welcome to a room if you want one. And I can show you the town as we walk there."

I accepted her offer and we walked together through Glastonbury, me with shoes now back on.

The town itself, although it has a worldwide reputation as a center of mystery and power, is physically very tiny. Really it is just one street, filled these days with New Age bookstores and shops selling crystals, incense, and other

---

27 Saint Manchan's poem, which describes the desire of the "green martyrs" to serve "the King who gives the sun its light" can be read in full at http://prayerfoundation.org/ancient__irish__monks__ poem.htm (retrieved September 11, 2009).

magical items. But something strange—some odd sense of other worlds—still hangs like a mist in its air.

At one end of the street that runs through it is the abbey, and on Magdalene Street, near the other, is Saint Mary's Church with its tapestry of saints and martyrs. In the center of the town there is a statue of Our Lady and the George and Pilgrim's Hotel, built to accommodate those on a mystical passage to the abbey. For those pilgrims, Saint George, the slayer of dragons, symbolized that their quest had come to an end and they had emerged from the dragon path to the place of their destination, as I now had. After what Cad had told me about the history of Glastonbury and its probable connections to the Grail, the significance of these names did not escape me.

Much bigger in its global influence than even the town itself, however, is the landscape of myths that surrounds it: Wearyall Hill, with its magical hawthorn that sprouted from Joseph's staff, stands just above it. Chalice Hill and the healing waters of Chalice Well look out across to the abbey, said to be the resting place of King Arthur. Nearby are the Mendip Hills, honeycombed with secret passages, and the stone circles of Stanton Drew, which date back 2,000 years before the arrival of Jesus. All of them hold Glastonbury like hands cupped around it, as if shielding some precious secret or offering the town up in prayer. I was reminded of the branches of the tree I had seen in the field in Wales, the image that had brought me here: of hands holding a chalice made from clouds.

Mel led me to her small guesthouse and found me a room. I unpacked the few things I had with me and took a shower, then lay down on my bed to relax. I fell asleep in the early evening and did not wake again until morning.

9

The Oaken Giants

One impulse from a vernal wood
May teach you more of man,
Of moral evil and of good,
Than all the ages can.

William Wordsworth,
"The Tables Turned"

𝕵 WOKE WITH a start. I had been too tired to really think about it yesterday or to ask many questions, but it seemed obvious now that there was a reason for Mel and I to meet. I had seen her three times—the hallmark of a good omen, according to Adam—and I felt certain that she was here to teach me *something*. Perhaps it might even be Adam's whereabouts. I dressed quickly and went down to the breakfast room.

Mel was making coffee when I arrived, and we sat down to a cup together. We chatted about nothing in particular for a while, and then she noticed the pouch around my neck that Cad had given me the day before.

"What do you have in your medicine bag?" she asked. "I know I shouldn't enquire, but I'm intrigued. You don't have to answer."

I was surprised that she would know about such things, and it gave me hope that my inklings now were correct and that she might know more about the matters unfolding than I had first thought.

A medicine bag is a package containing sacred objects used in the rituals of shamans. The typical items in such a bag might, for example, be animal teeth, stones, herbs, shells, bones, or tobacco, all of which have a special meaning or significance for the owner. The contents are not meant to be known or touched by anyone but the person who found them, as they represent, in a way, that person's soul and provide for his or her spiritual protection and healing. For this reason, it is usually considered inappropriate to ask what the contents are, and the person who carries it is not required to answer.

I didn't really consider it a medicine bag, however, but a gift from a friend that had a specific ritual purpose, so I didn't mind answering Mel's question. In fact, it gave me an opportunity to talk about Adam and the ceremony I hoped to perform for him with the contents of the pouch—a thanksgiving ceremony for finding him, as Cad had described it. I hoped as I spoke that the coincidences between Mel and me might be a greater sign of some special knowledge she had of Adam. Perhaps he had stayed here or she had passed him on the road as well when he made his own pilgrimage to the town?

While she seemed fascinated by Adam, however, there was no deeper glimmer of recognition—no sign or signal that she had ever met him.

"Your friend was a druid," she said simply when I finished.

Her conclusion took me by surprise because it was something I had never thought of before, although that now seems a bizarre oversight on my part. While it is true that Adam had been a healer and a philosopher and a man who knew well the souls of others, to me he was first and foremost a friend. To hear him described as a druid, therefore, carried the same disturbing fascination as discovering that anyone you have known for a long time had a secret interest or belonged to an arcane society that he had never revealed to you, but was obvious once it was pointed out—like being told that your father, brother, or friend was also a wizard, and then realizing *yes, of course*!

"It is a subject I know something about," she continued, "because I am studying for a master's degree in history with a special interest in religious practices like these. We also have many druids here in Glastonbury—both those who follow a genuine and ancient tradition and those who dance around in white costumes and think they are praising a goddess by doing so!"

She was making a distinction between the historical druids and druidism today (or what has come to be called neodruidism), which had its origins in seventeenth- and eighteenth-century inventions and the work of the romantic imagination.

The druids of history revered Celtic deities, while modern druids worship a variety of gods, even those of the Egyptians and Christians. Historical druids also followed a long path of learning (twenty years or more of intensive study, according to the Romans who wrote of them), while their modern counterparts earn courtesy titles based on their length of service to the Order rather than their study and dedication to the art.

The white dress of modern druids also stands in contrast to historical fact. Roman writers referred to the druids they met as "barbarian philosophers" dressed the same as other Iron Age people and made no mention of flowing robes.

Some of the beliefs of modern druids are also out of step with history. In particular, women were not allowed to become druids, although they now have a key role in many druidic circles. Nor did they worship the earth as a goddess, as their modern equivalents do, but worked with nature in all its forms without ascribing any gender to the forces they saw all around us.

Of these modern inventions and of druidry today, the British Museum writes diplomatically that "many of our popular ideas about the Druids are based on the misunderstandings and misconceptions of scholars 200 years ago. These ideas have been superseded by later study and discoveries."[28]

"The real druids were the priests and scholars of the Celts," said Mel. "They combined the roles of healers, seers, and holy men, as did your friend. They revered the natural world, as did your friend, and they held a particular respect for sacred trees and the groves in which they grew, as well as the hills, streams, plants, and elements, all of which they saw as the home of spirit.

"To druids, all of nature is alive—and more than this, divine. It presents us with omens, like the ones you have been following, which are insights into the mind of God. Your friend knew this, too, and left signs of his own for you to follow. And so I conclude that, whatever name you knew him by or whatever role he played for you, Adam was also a druid in the true sense of the word."

I could see her point, but I still found it hard to accept. I suppose my mind was filled with images of people "dancing around in white costumes," as Mel had described them, and nothing could be further from Adam's down-to-earth and

---

28 See the British Museum website: http://www.britishmuseum.org/ explore/highlights/article__index/d/the__druids.aspx (retrieved May 30, 2008).

unpretentious style. It amused me to think of him under moonlight in a pale robe making prayers to a Christian god he had little time for.

Nevertheless, I couldn't deny that Adam might well have had some connection to druidic practice. The word *druid* (*dryw* in Welsh) means "seer": one who looks through the veil into the spiritual world, an art which Adam was wholly familiar with.

According to Roman authors, not only was this seership practiced in Wales, but there was a druidic "university" there, on Anglesey (*Ynys Môn*), an island off its northwest coast, which druids from all over Europe would attend to undertake advanced and secret training. Pomponius Mela, the earliest Roman geographer, wrote of this training that it was conducted in caves and sacred forests before the Romans cut down the trees to destroy their power.

All of these things—the respect for nature, the reading of its signs to know the mind of God, the initiations in caves and forests—were familiar to me from my own work with Adam.

There was a further connection, too, in the origin of the Latin word for druid: *druides*—made up of *drus* for "oak" and *ides*, meaning "the son of." Druids were the sons of the oak, just as Adam had once described himself when introducing me to the folklore and healing of trees. The oak, in the "old language" he used for this, is known as *Arddam*; "Same as me," he had said, "*Arddam Dossa*, to be precise, which means 'most exalted of trees.'"

"We used to have real druids here too," Mel continued. "Perhaps we still have a few. They conducted their ceremonies in a grove not far from us. There are two very old oak trees there, which are all that now remain of a great tree-lined avenue leading to the tor. They date back to the time of Saint Joseph and are called the Oaks of Avalon: Gog and Magog.

"In the legends of Britain, Gog and Magog were ancient giants at the time of Brutus the Trojan, who invaded our island around 1103 BC. John Milton, the author of *Paradise Lost*, says that Albion (the ancient name for Britain) was then a land of giants, and that Gog and Magog were its fiercest protectors. But even they were eventually no match for Brutus.[29]

---

29 John Milton, *History of Britain*: "The Island, not yet Britain, but Albion, was in a manner desert and inhospitable, kept only by a remnant of Giants, whose excessive Force and Tyrannie had consumed the rest. Them Brutus destroies, and to his people divides the land, which, with some reference to his own name, he thenceforth calls Britain."

"Brutus built a city, which he called New Troy, until Lud erected defensive walls around it, and it then became known as Caer-Lud—the City of Lud, or, nowadays, London. It was here that Brutus took the defeated Gog and Magog.

"Brutus, however, went on to adopt the faith of the druids, seeing the errors in what he had done and, in some way, repenting for his sins. He died twenty-four years after his arrival in Britain, and his kingdom was then divided among his sons. The central part was given to Locrin and was called Loegria, eventually becoming England. Kamber inherited Kambria, now Wales, and Albanact took over Albania, now Scotland.

"In honor of the fallen defenders of Albion, however, the names of Gog and Magog were given forevermore to Glastonbury's two great oak trees, both of which are more than two thousand years old.

"They have a history that reaches back much further than this, though, because of the druids' practice of planting new oaks on the site of those that have fallen. The original Gog and Magog may therefore have been planted thousands of years before the two that now bear that name."

It was clear that Mel could not help me further with the whereabouts of Adam, but what she had just given me, I realized, was all the information I really needed. Chance had thrown us together so I could hear these words, and as I listened to her speak, it seemed to me that there could be no better place to perform the ritual I had in mind for Adam—the "man of oak"—than the site of these great oaken giants. Whatever happened after that was in the lap of the gods, and I would face it at the time.

I told Mel what I had in mind and she offered to show me the way to the trees, but I declined, knowing that this was something I wanted to or must do alone. And so, sometime in the afternoon, I set off to find Paradise Way, the romantically named approach to the ancient giants.

They were indeed vast, although frail with age and clinging to their lives. Their gnarled bodies and twisted limbs seemed to have taken on in shape the sights and experiences of their history. The faces of the people who had passed by them or stopped there to pray and all the other events of their time were recorded there, as if they had absorbed wisdom from the air, the sun, and, via their roots, from the earth itself. They were no longer just trees but a gallery of images and fragments making up a museum of life, with knowledge stored like sap in their oaken veins.

Around and nearby them a few red and white mushrooms grew, their bright colors standing in contrast to the greyish trunks of the trees. I began picking at one or two and then, almost without thinking, sank to the ground and sat cross-legged before the trees, drawn into a meditation. My eyes became unfocused, and I found myself gazing at the trees, dreaming myself into them and the evolution of the world that they had watched and been part of.

In places on their trunks and branches, pilgrims and penitents had left offerings. Beads, necklaces, crystals, ribbons, and painted stones adorned them, each of them a dream or a heartfelt wish absorbed by the tree and, through its boughs, carried up into the sky, where the sun illuminated it and the clouds would gather it into the prayerful world.

I was one with the memory of the trees, flowing like water through their season-rings and merging with the history contained there. I saw, as they had, the people who had made their prayers and offerings, and I knew what they longed for.

My mind drifted back to my first meetings with Adam and to another tree, an oak that he had asked me to sit before and gaze at it as I was now doing with the giants of this invisible forest. I was probably eight years old then, and sitting before the tree was a gentle form of initiation, Adam had said, into the power and wisdom of nature.

The tree that I sat in front of then had been struck by lightning and had a hole in its trunk that I was drawn to and compelled to sit within. It wrapped itself around me, and I floated like a breeze up through its branches and into the knowing universe, a pilgrim among the stars.

A thought went through my mind then as I recalled those events before these other oaks. I looked at them and silently asked my question. The response from nature was immediate: a robin—the messenger between worlds—flew into the branches of one of the trees and found a perch there. It sat looking at me for a few moments, as if calling me, then gathered the wind and flew past me. I had asked one of the trees if I might climb inside it and merge with it more fully, and its answer had been yes.

I walked over to it and began to climb. Several feet off the ground, there was a sort of natural platform where the upward-reaching boughs divided like an open hand. Reaching it, I looked down into the tree. It was hollow. I slipped inside and lowered myself to its leaf-strewn base.

It was quiet and dark within the body of the tree. Only the trunk separated me from the landscape outside, yet inside it was a different world. I felt a tingle of excitement run from the base of my spine to the base of my skull, but also a sense of safety at being present in a space where I knew I was nurtured and held. The tree became my cathedral and the darkening sky above me a blanket that was laid slowly over its entrance.

There was space enough inside to sit comfortably but not to do much else. I removed the pouch that Cad had given me and placed its contents in front of me, forming a circle of the petals and, in their center, the candle. Once lit, it gave off a mellow glow against the wood of the tree as the darkness gathered around me.

I sat for a few moments, breathing slowly and deeply, drinking in the power of the giant and letting it flow through me as I made my prayers for Adam: that I would find him or, if that were truly impossible, then at least the questions I had—about where he had gone, the journey we had shared, and about my own life and future choices— would finally be answered. It was a prayer I only half-completed, because all at once the perfect silence was shattered by a wild storm of noise.

It was not one sound in particular but a cacophonous blend: the screech of a thousand birds, a roar of voices, a million whispered longings, horns being blown against each other, a cascade of drums, the crash of hooves through undergrowth, the crackle of fires, screams, petitions, laughter, crying, incoherent words, stars falling to Earth and splitting the rocks of the landscape, the death of trees and the weeping of others as they mourned the loss of their fellows ... all of it at once, like a great shrill symphony.

It became deafening, a battering ram of sound that began to beat like a hammer on the outside of the tree, each blow sending vibrations through it that shook the trunk like a physical force.

Suddenly I knew what it was: I was part of the ancient memory of the tree and of all the sounds it had heard and absorbed across the ages: the sorrows and ecstasies of the people who had visited it in prayer, the animals that had moved around and through it, and finally, the fall of the forest that had surrounded it. I felt what the tree felt, knew what it knew, and became one with the burden of its knowledge. My body translated it through the DNA we shared so I could understand physically what it was to have seen and heard so much.

I knew as well that the tree I was a part of would soon die and that its great wisdom would be released to the soil to provide food for new growth, because this is how evolution takes place: through the flow of information to and from the Earth.

The trees of this forest had been cut down and sorrowfully accepted their fate as a sacrifice to this evolutionary process, and the day would come—sooner for us than for the trees—when we would return to the soil as well. This, at its basest, most primitive, and most glorious, was life. As the English poet Kathleen Raine wrote:

> Sensing us, the trees tremble in their sleep
> The living leaves recoil before our fires
> Baring to us war-charred and broken branches
> And seeing theirs, we for our own destruction weep.[30]

The world around me slowly returned to silence as the sounds of history receded. I breathed a sigh of melancholy and relief and, looking up, saw the eternal: the stars above me were beginning to pepper the sky.

"Peace at last," said a voice behind me.

I started. I had entered the tree alone. No one had been there and no one had joined me, so there should not have been another voice to hear. I snatched up the candle and shrank into the space behind me.

It was the eyes I saw first, glinting like silver in the candle glow, seemingly disembodied and floating in air, then the white hair that framed them, and finally the outline of a face with a mouth contorted into a grin, white teeth reflecting the light.

---

30 From "London Trees" in *Collected Poems* (Counterpoint, 1991).

"Adam?"

"More a dream of Adam—a wraith or a shadow," he replied. "We share a dragon path, you and I; a spirit trail, and your prayers have summoned me here. But I am not, of course, physically present. Still, a fine place you have chosen for this meeting!"

"A dream of Adam? So I am asleep, then?" I asked, sensing even then the strangeness or perhaps ridiculousness of asking a dream if I was dreaming it.

"We are all dreaming, and there is an unseen life that dreams us too," he answered. "That is how the world gets made: through our mutual dreams, like a tapestry woven from our wishes and wills. You are dreaming, but you are not asleep, so do not believe for one moment that this is not real, even if it is not."

His words made little sense but still, in some odd way, I understood them. I was dreaming and not dreaming. Whatever that really meant, the world chose to conspire with the illusion so that my back against the tree and the space around me felt real and solid enough, yet if I reached out to touch the man now addressing me, my hand passed through him like mist. If this was a dream, it was one dreaming me rather than the other way around. And yet it felt purposeful, like a shaman's journey, not meandering and surreal. I could interact with Adam, and he would respond in his own way, just as another person would, not as an aspect of my imagination.

"Why are you here?" I asked.

"I am here because you have conjured me—because your prayers have called me," he replied. "I am here because a dragon led me to this place, and this is where its fiery trail ends. I am here for resolutions and farewells and to persuade you that there is a world that demands your presence. Finally, I am here for the same reason that anyone is anywhere: because it is my choice. I wish to provide you with answers if you will hear them, so that your journey has purpose and clarity."

"Where have you been until now?" I continued.

"Good!" he said, clapping his hands together in his familiar way, which meant that action was called for. "Now we can go for a walk, and I will show you!"

It is tempting to say next that a door of some kind opened in the tree to allow us through, but that is not true or precise. What happened was that the tree unwrapped itself from around us, uncoiling like a serpent ... or a waking dragon. It moved to one side, and we stepped through its coils.

Adam seemed totally unperturbed by this, as if it were the most natural thing in the world that a tree should also be a snake. He shrugged his shoulders and looked at me. "Things in nature are not always as they seem," he said and began walking towards the fields.

I followed, glancing back once to see that the tree, whatever its true form, for now, at least, was once more a tree.

10

The Maid of the Hill

Where'er we tread, 'tis haunted, holy ground
No earth of thine is lost in vulgar mould
But one vast realm of wonder spreads around
And all the Muse's tales seem truly told.

Lord Byron,
"Canto the Second,"
Childe Harold's Pilgrimage

𝕬DAM WAS HUMMING beneath his breath, half-speaking and half-singing the words of a hymn:

> *And did those feet in ancient time*
> *Walk upon England's mountains green?*
> *And was the holy Lamb of God*
> *On England's pleasant pastures seen?*

"Do you know this song?" he asked. "Written by an old druid and inspired by a visit that the man Jesus once made to these parts, his idea being to create the New Jerusalem here, as told in the book of Revelation.[31]

"The Isle of Avalon is the wellspring of a great secret, you see. It was here that Jesus came with Joseph and his family after their flight from the old Jerusalem that had turned against love and crucified the savior that it had itself appointed. They didn't remain here for long, though,

---

31 "And Did Those Feet in Ancient Time" was written by William Blake (1757–1827) as the preface to his epic poem, *Milton* (1804). Music was added by C. Hubert H. Parry in 1916, and the work is best known today as the hymn "Jerusalem." Blake was involved in the eighteenth-century British revival of druidism and may also have been an archdruid of the Ancient Druid Order.

because they were spirited away soon afterwards to Wales, which became the birthplace of sin eaters.

"These events, as you might expect, are not unconnected, because Jesus, stripped down to the bones of the man, was himself a sin eater. You may remember the lines from Luke that Jesus utters when he is criticized for eating with sinners instead of the good men of God: 'I am not come to call the righteous but sinners to repentance,' because 'they that are in health have no need of a physician.'[32] With these words, Jesus reveals his purpose on Earth as a healer and devourer of sin.

"Of course, Jesus was simply preaching the facts of salvation, which the Welsh have always known, and so his words found acceptance with us as they had not in his own land. Wales became the home of sin eaters ... but it is Glastonbury where all of this began. Where better, then, for an old sin eater to make a final pilgrimage—or one who is starting out to make his first?

"The eating of sins had almost vanished from Wales when I was a young man," he continued. "It was the words of a stranger that kindled new warmth for the tradition ... among a few of us, at least. He knew how to read

---

32 Luke 5:31–32.

the Bible, you see, selecting his passages carefully to reveal its hidden truths, and he gave us new practices by which to experience and understand those truths."

I had read about the stranger in Adam's journal, and Cad had spoken at length about him, too. I was about to ask Adam who he was and where he had come from but he stopped me by putting his finger to his lips and nodding towards the landscape in front of us.

We were standing at the foot of the tor, but here, beneath moonlight, it was transformed. Lights danced around it, low in the air, and it had taken on a new shape, reminiscent of the old but for all the world now like that of a woman lying on her back with her head inclined towards us, watching us approach. In her body, consistent with the female form, there was an opening, a cave of sorts, in which a blue-white glow could be seen. We entered her and, for the second time on this journey, I was swallowed by the womb of the earth.

Over the centuries, many stories have been told of strange lights around the tor, including the testimony of a police officer who, in 1970, reported seeing luminous egg-shaped objects hovering in formation over the hill.

There are legends of passageways, too—tunnels beneath the earth. The most famous is an account by the Welsh

Saint Collen (AD 650), a former abbot of Glastonbury, who retired to a hermit's cell at the foot of the tor only to have his meditations disturbed by a strange and persistent visitor who invited him to enter a passage within it and meet the underworld king. Collen agreed and followed his guide into the earth, where he met Gwynn ap Nudd, the Lord of Hades. In prescient or presumptuous fear, the saint threw holy water over the king and immediately found himself alone on the hillside, never to know those mysteries again. Much of his remaining life was spent in sad reflection on that fact.

Others were not so lucky in their escape, however. Another legend tells of thirty monks who entered the hill through a secret passage that led from the abbey. Only three were ever seen again, two of them insane and one struck dumb and unable to speak of his experience.

In Celtic lore, the hill is Caer Sidi: the glass mountain or spiral castle where Cerridwen the Enchantress, owner of the magical cauldron of wisdom, makes her home and where the creative energies of the earth are felt most strongly. It was here that King Arthur entered on his quest for the Holy Grail, according to the Welsh poem "The Spoils of Annwn" in the Book of Taliesin. What he may have emerged with—and the truth, beyond its symbolic meaning, of what his discovery might mean for us today—is still in the hands of scholars.

All of this was far from my mind at the time, however. I reflected instead on what nature had revealed to me in a field in Wales, now seemingly so long ago:

> *There is a gateway that leads to a chalice and a*
> *hill. Adam will be found by passing through it.*

We were now standing in a passageway within this hill itself. It sloped gently downwards, and its walls were lined with crystals, which caught the light of the moon outside and cast it around us like showers of stars. Beneath our feet the ground was soil and stone, and Adam reached down to pick up something from there.

"Do you know what the Grail really is?" he asked.

"I expect you have heard all sorts of nonsense from Cad, who regards himself as a far greater scholar and much better read than I! Which is true, of course—but then, when did reading a book ever take the place of experience? I imagine at your age that you've probably read a few top-shelf magazines as well, and if they mean as much to you as actually knowing a woman, well, then..."

He left the point hanging and, perhaps a little embarrassed by his candor, cleared his throat and decided on a different approach. I found the friendly, ancient rivalry between Adam and Cad endearing, as well as Adam's slight discomfort at his over-enthusiastic run at Cad that had led him into a sexual analogy he was now unwilling to complete. It was like a father floundering sweetly to find a new tack in the belief that he might have gone too far, too soon in his explanation of the facts of life to his young son. I was glad to have Adam back.

"Now then," he began again, more formally this time, "there are those who say that the Holy Grail is a goblet that contained the blood of Christ, and there have been many fruitless wild hunts for it over the years by people who have become enchanted by this tin or pottery idol and spent their entire lives trying to find it.

"Others believe that the Grail is the blood of Christ himself: his sons and daughters and those of his several brothers and sisters named by Matthew.[33] It may be both or none of these things, but really it is this ... Hold out your hands in front of you."

---

33 Matthew 13:54–56: "And when [Jesus] was come into his own country, he taught them in their synagogue, insomuch that they were astonished, and said, Whence hath this man this wisdom, and these mighty works? Is not this the carpenter's son? Is not his mother called Mary and his brethren James, and Joses, and Simon, and Judas? And his sisters, are they not all with us?"

I did as he asked, and he placed in one of them a stone and in the other a pinch of dust. "These are the true Grail," he said, closing my hands around each in turn. "But it is also the cry of a newborn, a kiss between lovers, or the dream of a man or woman in love. It is a poem, a child, an idea, a prayer, or a hope … it is a metaphor—something that inspires us and gives us reason and cause. It points us towards freedom, to the natural cycle of things, and to the potential for new beginnings.

"The Grail is what whispers to our spirits of adventures yet to be lived. Trying to find it in the physical world is like a surgeon dissecting the body in the hope of finding a soul. It is never to be found, only to be known. That is its mystery and purpose."

I opened my hand and looked at the stone he had given me. It was small and smooth, yellow-gold, and shaped a little like a heart, although its appearance, I suspected, was irrelevant to the point he was making. The Grail, to Adam's mind, was the creative idea, the new dream that drives us and allows us to engage in play with the world. It was never to be taken literally but understood as a guide to the human spirit on its pilgrimage through the world as a seeker of truth.

"Whatever inspires you is your Grail," he said finally, quietly. I put the stone in my pocket, and we walked on.

It felt like we had traveled for a mile or more, going deeper as well as further into the earth with every step, when the tunnel opened out into a cave—or, really, I should say, into another world.

Curious beings sat around or clung to its walls. They were human-like but always there was something about them that made them not fully human. Some were thin and tall like insects but with bodies and features that resembled men and women; others were small and round like globes, with huge eyes that curved around their heads—fat children with grown-up faces. Around all of them there was a glow that also came from them, as if their breath itself was particles of light that clung to them in a cloud and grew brighter with each exhalation.

The strangest feature of this world, however, was that everything was inverted. Above me, the tops of trees grew downwards, surrounding a pool of water that hung in their center without spilling. Beneath me, birds flew across a sky that should have been grass and soil, among skittering clouds that stretched upwards to a sun below my feet. In this odd world I hung, suspended, "upside down," although it did not feel unnatural or strange but rather like I imagine an astronaut must feel when freed from gravity.

This was not the only inversion though. I looked at Adam, and where once there had been an old man, now there was a youth. He looked about my age, in his twenties, still recognizable as himself but how he would have been forty or fifty years ago. His once-white hair was fair, and his face was taut and firm around eyes that shone with the fire and passion of a young man: angry, ready, and confident of his place in the world.

I looked down at my hands and, by contrast, I was old. My hands were wrinkled and brown, the pores more open and the fingernails longer and thicker. My clothes were ill-fitting and hung from me, my body shape altered by age. I didn't feel any different and my body responded as it always had, but a change nonetheless had taken place. Even so, wisdom had not grown in me, and while I was willing to accept the changes, I found myself still looking to Adam for an explanation.

"It is nothing and it means nothing," he said. "It is just a conceit. You'll find the same changes taking place in the surface world before long, although it seems a lifetime away for you now. Things are a little different here, but the processes are the same. Still, nothing has really altered in you. Remember, you are dreaming.

"You asked me where I have been these last few years, and it is here, but really the question is *why* I have been where I am. I want you to meet someone now, and perhaps the answer to that will be clear."

He led me to the end of the cave where, in the center, a throne of carved oak was standing on a stage before a curtain of red velvet. A woman dressed completely in white sat there unmoving, a veil draped over her head so that her face could not be seen.

Beneath her oaken throne, a bowl of sage and bay leaves smouldered, surrounding her with aromatic smoke. In her hand she held a goblet of what I took to be mead, which she sipped from occasionally, drinking beneath the veil.

To her left there was a tall, thin man, dressed strangely, like a Victorian vaudeville compere, or master of ceremonies, in a black suit, sequinned red waistcoat, top hat, and spats. With a dramatic flourish, he bowed and threw his right arm out to his side, introducing the woman in white.

"Ladies and gentlemen, I give you the Maid of the Hill," he said as he backed away, still bowing, and left the stage through the curtains behind him to thunderous applause from his audience.

"Watch and listen," said the woman in white as the sounds of clapping died away. She began to screech and intone then—a wild, shrieking noise that, as it left her, became pictures projected onto the air in front of us. Her sounds made spirals, undulating like snakes, then congealing into images so that what I saw was words and forms all at once—information delivered in some strange hieroglyphic code or language of symbols that I could, nevertheless, understand.

> *The moon has had its fill of sin on Earth.*
> *The nature of man has changed*
> *And become unpalatable to the sin-eater moon.*
> *Once it was small and heartfelt concerns*
> *That it fed upon:*
> *Sorrows and regrets,*
> *Passions and yearnings,*
> *Acts which were still of love*
> *Though misguided or wrong.*
> *Now it is the loveless crimes*
> *Of the wicked few who are so lost and hungry for power*
> *That they will consume the world.*
> *They have poisoned their home and their souls*
> *And made themselves tasteless to the spirits.*
> *Without the moon to guide you,*

THE MAID OF THE HILL

The tides of man's fortunes will change
And the world will shiver in chaos.
The polluted souls of your leaders
Will express themselves
As the pollution of the earth.
The tides will rise and engulf them;
The flood will come,
And the sun will shine more brightly on the earth.
Then, through God's illumination,
Those who have sinned will be transformed
From matter to spirit.
Those without true hearts,
Who have forgotten their purpose and origin
And fallen amongst illusion
Will be transformed,
Ravaged by waves and plague.
It will be an end and a beginning,
For Albion and Eden will rise again
from this great cleansing,
And Earth will become a paradise once more
For the righteous few
Who remain
Aware
And awake
To love.

The stream of word-pictures ended, and the woman before me fell silent. The compere stepped back onto the stage and began to clap, throwing up his arms to encourage the others present to do so also.

"Once again, ladies and gentlemen, the Maid of the Hill!" he said, and the cave went wild with applause. "Thank you v'much!" he responded, in a poor impression of Elvis, and with that, he bowed to her again and left the stage.

Such strange behavior on the part of otherworldly beings, although it seems odd to us, is apparently quite common. The myths and fairy tales of Europe tell of curious reversals, words, and gestures on the part of fairies and elementals that are almost understandably human but not quite, as if they are somehow a pastiche of what humans would do and say.

A modern version of the same strange behavior is reported by alien abductees such as Whitley Strieber who, in his book *Communion* (Harper, 2008), describes the beings he encountered as acting in a bizarre but still human-like way in surroundings that were almost circus or carnival-like. Nobody really knows why these beings behave in the ways they do, but odd encounters that are unnerving but also comical are quite consistent in literature and personal accounts.

"The oracle is a channel for the earth," said Adam, "nothing more. She does not possess 'supernatural' powers any more than you or I or anyone else. In fact, every experience—indeed, if there is anything to experience at all—cannot, by definition, be supernatural, or 'beyond nature,' because it is part of our being to perceive it, and we are a part of nature. No, her abilities are entirely natural but more developed, that is all. And so, by simply watching the signs of nature, anyone can verify what she says. She speaks in poetry, but her message is clear: 'So perish monuments of mortal birth, so perish all in turn, save well-recorded worth.'[34]

"In plainer language: there is a change coming to the earth. It will be brought about by your leaders—the people you have been a little too anxious to give your power to and who have used that power for their own ends.

"This change cannot be averted. It will begin with a flood and then pestilence, famine, and cold: what the oracle has called the new plagues of Egypt. She means all of this literally, by the way, and all of it, she says, is inevitable; there is nothing that any of us can do to make it otherwise.

---

34 From Lord Byron, "Canto the Second," *Childe Harold's Pilgrimage.*

"That is why we remain here—not to escape what must be or to prevent it but to charge the land so its dragon paths shine like beacons for those who are prepared to act for their own salvation."

He turned to the center of the cave, and I followed his gaze. All of its inhabitants were standing, hands joined, their heads tilted backwards, looking up to the world above them. Now, though, instead of the half-human forms they once possessed, they were creatures of light with no human features at all. Shining and translucent, they prayed together, and from their words luminous orbs formed and drifted upwards through the roof of the cave as food for the earth. With chants that were soothing like lullabies, they gave their life force to a world they were not even part of.

"Some of the oracle's predictions are bizarre, even to me," said Adam. "It is hard to fathom how the world is capable of such change or why such terrible events may come to pass. She says also that within thirty years people will be more like machines than human beings, and that what we knew as information will be noise.

"All of this is alien to me—and yet she cannot be wrong since she is a channel for the earth itself, and we can rightly expect that the greater mind of our planet knows what is, what has been, and what is to come.

"But anyway, your question is answered, and your search is over. This is where I have been and why I remain. When I came to you, I said that one of my reasons was to persuade you that the earth requires your presence, so while your search may be over, your quest is not. Knowing what is to come, you must return to the world above us and make your choices. Join with others, create a community of souls, and together learn the old ways, because these are what will sustain you in your lifetimes. That is your mission now."

We walked back in silence for the rest of our journey through the crystal tunnel to the place we had entered. "This is our goodbye," Adam said suddenly then. "You were a child when we first met, but we have known each other for many years since then, and we are both older now. It is time to put away childish things and take our responsibilities seriously in these puzzling and questful times. You have a life to be part of, adventures to live, and, as you see, preparations to make. Remember: you are dreaming, and visit me in your dreams sometime."

I looked down at my hands, and my body was normal again. Having stepped out of the cave, I was a young man once more. When I looked back, Adam was gone, and the tor was once again just a tor. I closed my eyes and felt the night air on my face—the breath of a fragile planet whose future, however far-off and distant it seemed to me now, was already known to the gods who watched over it.

When I opened my eyes again, it was to darkness. It took me a few moments to get my bearings, but then I realized that I was back inside the tree. From the position of the moon and stars above me, it seemed that only minutes had passed despite the apparent hours I had spent in the tunnels beneath the earth. "Remember: you are dreaming," Adam had said, and yet it felt more real than that.

The candle had gone out, and I fumbled for it in the shadows of the tree, then reached into my pocket for matches. Instead, my hand found something small and smooth. I lit the candle and studied it. It was a stone, yellow-gold and heart-shaped.

Some years later, when the world had taken on more of the form that Adam had predicted, I would place it on my altar, where it now remains. Though it has faded, on the back of it, in a certain light, a figure eight is still just visible.

11

The Dragon's Labyrinth

❖❖ And he took me up in spirit to a great
and high mountain
And he shewed me the holy city.

Revelation 21:10

THE SUMMIT OF Glastonbury Tor is the town's highest point. From it, on a clear day, you have a view of Britain for miles around, including the Black Mountains of Wales, way off in the distance, where my journey had begun.

It was not a clear day though. A mist hung over the meadow, making the air a blanket of white. A strange daylight filtered through it, as if tiny prisms of water had been sewn into this blanket of mist. They sparkled momentarily, then faded as I passed through them. It was a landscape the Celts would have entered with caution, aware that mist contains the kingdom of the fey, the spirit-folk who lead unwary travelers to their immaterial fates.

Above me, visible through the smoky vapors, the retiring moon and the rising sun both hung in the sky, one of them milky and blurred, the other pale and yellow like a drop of paint on an artist's watercolor.

The mist itself settled at just above head height, so it was possible to jump up and, just for a moment, to be part of the clear air before gravity made its demands on the body and I fell to the earth again. Adam would have said that the field had become a betwixt-and-between place with its watery surface the threshold between two worlds: the silent, closed-in realm of the clouds that had gathered there and the bright world above it, where the sun god offered warmth and illumination and the moon smiled down on human frailty.

I had spent an uncomfortable night inside the oak. While it was fine to sit up in, there was no room to stretch out or lie down, and there was only its hard trunk to use as a pillow. My contortions and the chill of night had kept me awake for most of it, and my thoughts and brief dreams were of Adam, the oracle, and her predictions for our planet.

Create community and learn the old ways, Adam had said, "because these are what will sustain you in your lifetimes." I knew that he meant it literally and that by "the old ways" he was not referring to the magical crafts of our ancestors but to something more practical: their survival skills and their knowledge of nature.

In the coming world that the oracle had described, we would need these skills in order to provide for ourselves, because no government would be able to do so. And yet how many of us know how to build shelters, make clothes, grow food, or even create fire? We had forgotten the very basics of life, seduced by the ease of our technologies and a society that seemed—but only seemed—to do it all for us. A change was coming, though, where these false comforts would no longer exist, certainly not in their current form, and we would need to find another way, joining with others on a more human level to do so.

In this new world, I realized, my own "skills," such as they were—and those of many others—would be useless. What good is a university education, after all, or a business empire, in a world where there are no goods to sell and no way to distribute them to a society that had become fractured and chaotic? The brightest PhD student, salesman, celebrity, or CEO would be lost in such a world. But a woodsman, a gardener who could grow plants and make foods and medicines from them, or the poorest man in the world who at least knew how to make fire ... they would be our saviors.

These are the thoughts that occupied me until I had emerged from the tree at dawn, intending to climb the tor as the final part of my journey. Something about the meadow scene in front of me, however—some vague memory or odd feeling of recognition or déjà vu—stopped me in my tracks. Then I remembered Adam's journal and one of the entries he had written: "The moon is high and white, casting a silver light through the mist, but it is daytime too and the sun is up: a curious mixture of light and shade, a crucial hour, no doubt."

I was looking at the landscape that Adam had seen in a dream, an image that had called him to this place, just as it had called me.

"I have a curious feeling in my dream, as well: as if someone is watching me, standing behind me, and observing my journey." He had written these words, too, and with a sudden shock, I realized that *I* was the person he had sensed there, the unseen observer who had been following the path he had taken. He had dreamed this moment, too, where I would be his witness once again to this, his final journey.

I thought about what Cad had said: dragon paths create parallel universes, dreams create reality. The whole world, it seemed to me now, was a great web of connections where everyone was somehow related and we are each leaders and followers, authors and players in a story that has been told throughout time.

I made my way to the tor, the sacred hill that has been walked by millions down the ages, each of us invisibly connected by our dreams, needs, intentions, or a calling that defied understanding but was more than just a desire to stand on the summit of a hill. What really linked us was a belief in something more than a known and ordered world.

In certain lights, it can be seen that terraces are carved into the tor that form a single pathway that winds seven times around its slopes, a labyrinth that encircles it. Nobody yet has exactly dated this pathway, but they are sure that it was made in prehistory; some say the second or third millennium BC, when the lake villages of Glastonbury were founded. Remains of graves discovered at the summit date back to the fifth and sixth centuries, suggesting that it was a place of power then at least.

This ritual path around the hill—the Pilgrim's Path, as it has come to be called—has the same pattern as the ancient labyrinth of Knossos, a design received by oracle-priestesses in their dreams of Ariadne, the "utterly pure" snake goddess of fertility and inspiration.[35]

Sacred to the moon, its function at Knossos was to hold the minotaur, a creature half-human, half-bull, which was eventually killed by Theseus, aided by Ariadne, who gave him a thread—a clew, or clue—so he could find his way back out.

---

35 Ariadne, according to some scholars, is a derivation of the word *ari-hagne*: "utterly pure."

Psychologists who have taken their inspiration from Greek myths see such paths as symbols. By walking the labyrinth, they say, we go deeper into ourselves and discover the beast within us: a primal force which, unconquered, will lead us into sin and self-destruction, as we are always tempted by death. They call it *thanatos*—the desire for endings. We tame the beast by walking the maze, led by the more placid and contemplative energies symbolized by the moon, the "first sin eater." Our spiral passage is a journey of the soul.

The Celts had a similar view. To them, spirals were coiled serpents: the natural energies of the earth. The Glastonbury maze was a dragon path, as Adam had described it in his journal, to be walked with the intention of lifting the veil between worlds.

At the top of the tor, at the center of the labyrinth, there is a tower, a fragment of an ancient church built in the twelfth century and dedicated to Saint Michael, the ruler of archangels and slayer of dragons. To some, Saint Michael, the "Lord of Angels," is another name for Jesus, so perhaps there was a deeper meaning to this church, given the history of the town that surrounds it and its connections to the Grail.

In 1275, in any case, the church crashed, ruined, to the ground, and another was built to replace it. The tower of that second church is all that now remains. Markings on it show the saint with weighing scales by which to measure the sins and the souls of the dead, and beside him is Saint Bridget.

Michael, the bearer of light, revealer of mysteries, and guide to the other world, is the Christian successor to Lugh, the Celtic light-bringer, while Bridget was originally Bride, the goddess of poetic inspiration, fire, the hearth, and the sun. The symbolism, then, is complete: by walking the dragon path and slaying the monsters we find along our ways, we arrive at the center purified, in a place where we are closest to the sun—the illumination of the first god—where Michael, his foot upon the serpent, signifies the end of our quest.

The entrance to the Glastonbury labyrinth is in Wellhouse Lane, near the site of the Chalice Well, where I had first entered the town—another circle completing itself: the serpent eating its tail. To walk it, you must gather your intention and prepare to enter another world, otherwise it is like traveling any path that has no particular sense of meaning or purpose to it. However, by slowing down to the pace of nature, breathing slowly and deeply, and by maintaining a gentle awareness of your inner states, it is possible to change your consciousness so that walking the labyrinth becomes a form of meditation. At one with the labyrinth, it forgets you are there, so you blend with it, and what is separate and human within you diminishes. The labyrinth begins to walk *you*.

I paused at the fallen stones that are the entrance to it, breathing in the mist that surrounded me, then took my first step. The journey to the top would take about two hours at the pace I intended, giving me time to reflect on my experiences these last few days and take guidance, if it were offered, from the spirits of the hill.

"There are many times when a pilgrimage may be useful to settle the mind and restore the soul," Adam had written. "But certainly there are two: when a man is first starting out in life and needs to know his path, and when he is nearing the end of it."

This journey had begun for me just as he said: because I was at a place in my life where I needed to find clarity. What surprised me now, however, was that I hadn't really considered my personal needs or the questions I had brought with me since my first arrival at Cad's. My immersion once more in the philosophy and arts of the sin eater had consumed me instead, with its continuing adventure encompassing the mysteries of the Grail, the legends of the kings and saints of Britain, and my encounters with dream worlds, spirit healers, signs and omens, and the laments of the sorrowful dead.

Perhaps my questions—or the questions that anyone might ask of their lives—were less important than I'd thought, and it is really the quest, the adventure itself, that calls us. As soon as we feel that we belong, that there is a mystery for us to solve, and that the world is not as mapped and mundane as we are told, we come alive again to its strange poetry of magic and beauty. Perhaps this was what had really been missing from my life: a sense of passion and the desire to be part of something still unfolding and unsolved. In a way, it came back once again to purpose, something that Adam had spoken of many times in our past adventures. To know one's purpose—to commit to it, follow it, and take pleasure from it—was, for the sin eater, the most important thing we can do.

"To be bound by purpose is to be free," he had once said. "People often get this confused and believe that freedom results from having no commitments or ties at all. But this just gives rise to a meandering life—to chaos, errors, and self-obsession—and, ultimately, to regrets.

"It is true, of course, that we should not give our power away to others or curtail our rights and freedoms by binding ourselves to their intentions for us, because that results in a life unlived. But it is equally true that what each man needs is a clew: a solid core, a thread, or a philosophy he can return to—something to believe in and a reason to be. With this, he knows himself and has a safe harbor to return to where he can find shelter when the storms of the world besiege him. Without purpose, we are lost.

"And the greatest purpose of all? To love. Even those who have no idea of what they came here to do, if they find what sets them aflame, it will reveal the meaning in life for them."

Purpose, however, can also find us. Or, at least, that is how it now seemed to me from my experience of this journey so far. We do not always have to search frantically for meaning or reasons as long as we stay open and available to the whispers of spirit: the wind in the trees, the wisdom of the stream, or the language of the clouds—to the signs of nature and the information that flows through it.

What fires our souls and sings to our hearts is where purpose can be found. By recognizing the two pillars of wisdom that life's experience offers us—*follow your bliss* and *do no harm*—we steer a course through the storms that Adam had spoken of, and, inevitably, on this journey of the spirit, we reach a destination that is fulfilling and uniquely ours. We return home, the ultimate goal of the pilgrim.

The questions that I had first brought to my journey revolved around functions: what to do next, where to go in my life, what tasks to perform or what status to aim for—all of the hypnotic persuasions, prohibitions, and expectations of a society where I needed to "make something of myself," find a career, pay my bills, become a consumer of its views, a member of its circle, and an upright citizen ... and so give up my power to others so they could determine the course of my life. Through subtle shifts of awareness, however, I had arrived at a deeper understanding of the world I belonged to and the conviction that I owed a debt of responsibility not to a society whose rules I had never agreed to abide by but to myself and my planetary home.

With my footfalls on the dragon path, I had learned more about what my purpose was—and what it was not. It was to find a community that I wanted to be part of, not join one that held no allure for me or respect for people like me who rejected its mainstream beliefs and which, in a few decades in any case, would have reached the end of its viability as a result of those beliefs—according to the oracle, at least.

A realization like this was, in Adam's words, "the goal of the pilgrimage." The reason for such a journey, he had written, is not "to go further and further afield but to return home," to arrive back where we started. It is not a one-way journey but a circle that completes itself. "The point, along the way, is to open our eyes ... to change ourselves because of the mission we have undertaken ... so we see the Garden we stand in"—to find our fire and commit to something we can believe in. We are "not running away but running towards."

In the dream that Adam recorded in his journal, he envisioned a gateway at the summit of a hill, and that is what Saint Michael's tower is. It stands open at the center of the labyrinth and has an entrance to a small sheltered area where pilgrims have stopped to carve their marks before passing through to the other side.

I looked for Adam's among them—the *8* and the *B*—but they were not there. Somehow it didn't really matter, though. It was a dream that led me to Glastonbury and a dream where Adam's destiny and the future of us all had been revealed. We spend a third of our lives dreaming, and this information is potent, real, and has purpose. It had provided me with adventure, meaning, and the seeds of a new future. What would have been added to this by seeing "proof" of Adam's presence in a carving on a stone?

I looked out over the landscape, with the mist below me like a distant sea, and imagined the Isle of Avalon as it had once been and might be again when the waters rise up around us, with the tor as the only beacon for those who needed to find their way home.

It is an interesting word, home. The American poet Robert Frost described it as "the place where, when you have to go there, they have to take you in"—a place of begrudging safety. But I hoped it was more than that. Home is where we are welcomed, loved, and belong. It may have no fixed meaning in time or space, but we know it still from the feelings it invokes in us and the tenderness we receive there from others.

Wales and the Black Mountains on the horizon before me with the village of Ullingswick in their foothills were where I had grown up and first met Adam, but they were no longer my home. The world was my home now. It was there that new beginnings and other adventures awaited me.

I turned to walk back to Saint Michael's tower and make my own pilgrim's mark, but something stopped me. My eye had found a familiar sign on the outside of the gateway near its base: an *8* and a *B*. I smiled and scratched my own mark beside it: H8.

Should your journeys ever take you to Glastonbury, perhaps you will find these marks there, beneath the image of Saint Michael, the slayer of serpents, at the end of a dragon path.

I made my way back down the tor and, an hour or so later, collected my things from Mel's. I thanked her for her hospitality and, with little ceremony, walked out in sunlight from Glastonbury, a pilgrim once more under still-hopeful skies.

> *Any action we make might be a pilgrimage,*
> *whether the journey takes a moment or a lifetime—*
> *because we are always acting ... To be pilgrims is*
> *what we came to this world to do. It is our destiny.*
>
> Adam Dilwyn Vaughan (1901–)

The Good and Bad Seeds

Things fall apart; the center cannot hold;
Mere anarchy is loosed upon the world,
The blood-dimmed tide is loosed, and everywhere
The ceremony of innocence is drowned ...
Surely some revelation is at hand;
Surely the Second Coming is at hand.

William Butler Yeats,
"The Second Coming"

How do we know sin? How do we avoid it? From whom do we take our inspirations in this world, where all things are available and we are taught only to value ourselves?

Imagine that you have a garden in which you have planted the seeds of various fruits and vegetables, without ever looking to see what they are. Eventually all of them will grow if they are fed and watered sufficiently, but still, you do not know what your harvest will be.

Some produce plants that are nourishing when we eat them. They give us strength and enable us to live richer and happier lives. Others yield fruits we do not like or that make us ill and may even be poisonous. The first thing, then, is to pay attention to what you are planting!

But even if you are a careless gardener, all is not lost, because we can also recognize good and bad seeds by the effects of their fruits on us if we at least observe what we receive by eating them. And, once we know this, we have choice. We can continue to plant the bad as well as the good and to eat all the fruits we produce even though we are sickened by some of them. Or we can plant only good seeds from now on and give more of our soil and our souls to them so they grow stronger and yield more fruit.

And so it is with sin. If we approach our lives with purpose and pay attention to our actions and the results they produce, sooner or later we will learn what is useful and what impoverishes our souls.

In short: to know sin, we must watch ourselves and be guided by what our actions achieve. We do not need to be told by others what sin is or how to avoid it because the good gardener is a citizen of nature. Through his experience, he learns to plant only good seeds and tend to them wisely so they grow strong in the sunlight and add beauty to the world.

As a species, human beings have not been especially adept at knowing the difference between good and bad seeds or taking care of our garden, Earth. We know that now.

However, in the 1980s, when my pilgrimage took place, the oracle's messages were difficult to understand because they seemed so pessimistic and at odds with the times. Western civilization was riding a wave of good fortune then, with new wealth and opportunities and such an obsession with the self and immediate gratification, and so little thought for the future, that the media would later come to call this age Generation Me. It was the era of yuppies and Wall Street, with its mantra of greed is good. Anything—by any means and without conscience or consequences—seemed possible.

As bizarre as it sounds now, the world had not heard of the environment, or else we cared little about it. For another twenty years, America, the world's greatest polluter, would be concerned more about profits than its impact on the earth.[36] Now the phrases "credit crunch," "recession,"

---

36 BBC News, June 2, 2002: "The world's largest polluter, America, has recently not backed pollution treaties to reduce car emissions or petrol consumption. The US alone accounted for 36.1% of worldwide greenhouse emissions in 1990" (http://news.bbc.co.uk/1/hi/world/asia-pacific/2024265.stm; accessed June 11, 2008). BBC News, February 14, 2002: "The US contains 4% of the world's population but produces about 25% of all carbon dioxide emissions. By comparison, Britain emits 3%—about the same as India, which has 15 times as many people" (http://news.bbc.co.uk/1/hi/world/americas/1820523.stm; accessed June 11, 2008).

and "global (by which we really mean Western) economic crisis" are familiar to everyone, and global warming has become the theme of our age. Awareness comes late, however, and we cannot immediately go back to the world we once knew.

Those who are making apocalyptic predictions now are not oracles but scientists. One of them is James Lovelock, who, more than thirty years ago, made the discovery that our planet has an intelligence by which it controls our environment to keep it fit for life. He called his discovery the Gaia Hypothesis, and it is now widely accepted. Lovelock believes that through our actions, the Gaia system is failing, and climate change cannot be reversed.

"The world has already passed the point of no return for climate change ... civilization as we know it is now unlikely to survive," he says. "Before this century is over, billions of us will die, and the few breeding pairs of people that survive will be in the Arctic, where the climate remains tolerable."

The best scenario for the rest of us, he says, unless we form sustainable small communities and learn the survival skills of our ancestors, is that we will become "a broken rabble led by brutal war lords."[37]

---

37 *The Independent*, January 16, 2006: "Environment in crisis: We are past the point of no return" at http://www.independent.co.uk/

His predictions are gloomy, but it is just as well that we know them, because then we have the power to make choices and can prepare for our new futures.

The rising tides, wild weather, and intemperate climates that global warming brings means that the cycles of nature will be disrupted, and we are already seeing evidence of "the new plagues of Egypt" that Adam spoke of. Malaria-carrying mosquitoes and biting insects are finding new habitats, for example, as the earth warms up and conditions become more humid. Professor Roger Wotton, a biologist at University College London, suggests how things may progress. "The dramatic series of events that included the Nile turning to blood and a plague of frogs are explicable as natural phenomena," he says, as a result of weather conditions not unlike our own now.[38]

---

environment/environment-in-crisis-we-are-past-the-point-of-no-return-523192.html (accessed June 11, 2008) and *The Independent*, January 16, 2006: "James Lovelock: The Earth is About to Catch a Morbid Fever That May Last as Long as 100,000 Years" at http://www.independent.co.uk/opinion/commentators/james-lovelock-the-earth-is-about-to-catch-a-morbid-fever-that-may-last-as-long-as-100000-years-523161.html (accessed June 11, 2008). Lovelock's new book, *The Revenge of Gaia*, was published by Penguin in 2006.

38 *The Times*, December 15, 2007: "Plagues of Egypt 'caused by nature, not God'" at http://www.timesonline.co.uk/tol/comment/faith/article3053571.ece (accessed September 22, 2009).

All of this was predicted by the oracle, and as odd as it may seem, some of her stranger predictions have also been borne out by events. One of them was that within thirty years (that is, by about 2014), people will be more machine than human and "what we knew as information will be noise." In fact, by 2007 governments in many countries were already launching health initiatives because people were spending so little time in nature or even in the "real world" but were instead plugged in to the Internet, television, video games, mobile phones, and virtual reality, leading to what they saw as an epidemic of obesity and ill health. These inventions were unheard of in the 1980s, and all of them are based on information that has become so overwhelming that it has, indeed, become noise.

Finally, there is the oracle's curious prediction that the conditions we are now experiencing have arisen because the moon—"the first sin eater"—has withdrawn from the earth in distaste at the changing nature of the world. For years, I have taken this as a metaphor: that our governments will lose sight of their morals and lead us into wars and more frenzied profit-seeking to the detriment of our planet—as, indeed, the history of recent years suggests. But that may not be all there is to it.

There is also an idea, now current among scientists, that the moon may have a more practical role to play in our understanding of the changes on Earth. According to a NASA-funded study, for example, "insights into Earth's climate may come from an unlikely place: the moon ...

"Scientists looked at the ghostly glow of light reflected from Earth onto the moon's dark side. During the 1980s and 1990s, Earth bounced less sunlight out to space. The trend reversed during the past three years, as the Earth appears to reflect more light toward space."[39]

The light of Earth—in effect, the energy given off by we who live here—is increasing, but seemingly no longer to the taste of the moon, which is more or less what the oracle said.

The predictions made all those years ago, then, have in many ways come to pass, some more quickly than even the oracle imagined. Our future now lies in forming the communities that Adam spoke of, learning the ways of our ancestors, and taking a greater, more loving, and more respectful interest in the world.

---

39 See "Scientists Look at Moon to Shed Light on Earth's Climate" at http://www.nasa.gov/centers/goddard/news/topstory/2004/0528earthshine.html (accessed June 5, 2007).

Some of this may already be happening, as good seeds are planted to counteract the bad. One recent development, for example, small in itself but encouraging nonetheless, is the resurgence of the tradition of sin eating.

Though previously considered defunct in its original form, traces of the sin-eating custom have continued, and if you attend any funeral you will encounter them, notably in the wake customs of Ireland, Wales, and Scotland, where food and drink are laid out in the presence of the corpse to symbolize the purity of the soul within the deceased body.

Other than these remnants, however, little is known about the true custom or the original sin eaters: who they were or what they believed, or about sin eating as it was first conceived and practiced. There are even some who question the very existence of these guardians of the soul.

The historian Wirt Sikes is one. He wrote about a meeting of the Cambrian Archaeological Association at Ludlow in August 1852, for example, where Matthew Moggridge of Swansea spoke about the custom.

"When a person died," said Moggridge, "his friends sent for the sin eater of the district, who on his arrival placed a plate of salt on the breast of the defunct, and upon the salt a piece of bread. He then muttered an incantation over the bread, which he finally ate, thereby eating up all the sins of the deceased. This done, he received his fee of 6d (sixpence) and vanished as quickly as possible from the general gaze; for, as it was believed that he really appropriated to his own use and behoof the sins of all those over whom he performed the above ceremony, he was utterly detested in the neighbourhood; regarded as a mere Pariah, as one irredeemably lost."

"Such is the testimony," says Sikes. "I venture no opinion upon it further than may be conveyed in the remark that I cannot find any direct corroboration of it as regards the Sin-eater, and I have searched diligently for it. The subject has engaged my attention from the first moment I set foot on Cambrian soil, and I have not only seen no reference to it in Welsh writings, but I have never met any unlettered Welshman who had ever heard of it. All this proves nothing, perhaps; but it weighs something."[40]

In 2008, during research for a television documentary based on my book *The Sin Eater's Last Confessions*, I contacted St. Fagans National History Museum in Cardiff, Wales, to see if they could shed any further light on the practice. The curator, Emma Lile, was almost as dismissive as Sikes. "The practice has long disappeared in Wales," she

---

40 Wirt Sikes, *British Goblins: Welsh Folk-lore, Fairy Mythology, Legends and Traditions* (London, 1880).

said. Her response did, at least, suggest that it was a custom that once existed, in contrast to Sikes' conclusions, but the general consensus was that sin eating had vanished from the cultural landscape somewhere in the mid-1800s.

Chance intervened to change that, however, when, quite by accident, I came across a contemporary sin eater as part of the same documentary research. "I provide spiritual comfort to the recently bereaved," he told me, "following teachings from my grandparents, who did the same. I'm not any sort of village wise man; I simply carry out a small ritual over a recently departed brother or sister. My [Welsh] grandmother was the person from whom I learned this. She taught me no strict ritual, more a set of actions, very simple, and a few words to say. I think I may be just a faint shadow and relic of something much bigger; a bit like an old gravestone with the writing gone, or a burial mound: a lump in a field or a tumulus on an OS map."

Although SW, as he asked me to call him, felt that sin eating was mostly lost to the modern world, the fact that he is here at all is comforting: someone, at least, is taking care of the soul by planting good seeds for the future of our world and its regeneration from small shoots and new beginnings.

For me, two mysteries remain from the pilgrimage I embarked upon all those years ago. The first is the identity of the stranger who had so inspired Cad and Adam and who, in some way, contributed to the adventure I shared with them. I have carried out research over the years and considered many ideas about who he may have been. There is one that I return to.

There was a man—a wisdom teacher from Europe—now long dead, who fits the description Cad gave of him. In 1921 and 1922, when Cad and Adam would have been at an appropriate age, this teacher made a pilgrimage of his own to western Europe to give demonstrations of his work in cities, including London.

London to Wales is a distance of less than two hundred miles, and it is therefore conceivable that he may also have traveled there and, by chance, met two young men eager to know more of his philosophy, which was so in keeping with their own.

This teacher believed, as Adam did, that the body, mind, and spirit were one and must be kept in balance for us to know spiritual health and equilibrium. Both he and Adam also referred, in their unique ways, to Bible passages to demonstrate their conclusions about the soul and the possibility of its redemption.

Both also taught ways to increase our spiritual energy and focus it to find purpose, avoid wasted efforts, and wake up to a better world. The stranger's methods included practices and movements that were like Adam's in many ways, and he introduced an exercise he called the Stop, where the student, as Cad more or less described it, would stop what he was doing on a certain command and then calmly observe his mental, emotional, and physical states so he could better understand and "re-member" himself.

"You must realize," this teacher said, "that each man has a definite repertoire of roles which he plays in ordinary circumstances ... but put him into even slightly different circumstances and he is unable to find a suitable role, and for a short time he becomes himself."

One of his ideas was that we are "food for the moon," just as Cad related it. The moon feeds on our energies, sins, and souls. An aware and awake man, however, has a shot at freedom and can know his truth and purpose while he is alive so that he does not become one of the sorrowful dead, "ill-met by moonlight."

According to the stranger, however, the number of people who would actually arrive at this awareness was just "five of twenty of twenty."

Only twenty percent of us will break out from our habits and conditioning, that is, and consider the possibility of a greater freedom, and of these, only twenty percent will do anything about it. Just five percent of those who remain will find their freedoms.

The mathematics of this equation are not hopeful. It means that 0.2 percent of people—or two in a thousand—stand any real chance of enlightenment. For the most part, then, the world is led by people who are undeveloped and unevolved: bad seeds giving rise to the conditions we experience today.

There is a great deal of correspondence between this teacher's philosophy and Cad's descriptions of the work that he and Adam did with him, but I still hesitate to reveal his name. There is some piece of evidence missing—or perhaps it is a lack of conviction on my part—that means I am not certain enough to announce it. He is, however, well-known, and research of your own will reveal him to you from the clues I have given.

For me, however, the greatest mystery of all still remains: what really became of Adam. It is one that I imagine time has now solved, for he was an old man when I knew him, and a quarter of a century or more has passed since the events of this book. No one can live forever, at least in this physical world.

Although I made further visits to Wales and met with Cad again, I returned only briefly to Hereford, the place of my childhood adventures with Adam. Shortly after my return from Glastonbury, in fact, my family moved away from the town, and my association with it was mostly lost.

Nobody can say with certainty, then, where Adam has gone, but I have an answer that satisfies me—at least until another is found. It was given to me in an oaken dream one Glastonbury day, of a man who had found a community of spirit where he was needed and belonged in a way that he may never have experienced as a sin eater on the edges of our society.

Somewhere outside of time, Adam has found his home and taken his place among the Merlins and immortals of a new Camelot, young and strong and at one with the world he loved.

> *May you continue to inspire us:*
> *To enter each day with a generous heart.*
> *To serve the call of courage and love*
> *Until we see your beautiful face again*
> *In that land where there is no more separation,*
> *Where all tears will be wiped from our mind,*
> *And where we will never lose you again.*[41]

❖ ❖ ❖

---

41 John O'Donohue, "On the Death of the Beloved," from *To Bless the Space Between Us: A Book of Blessings* (Doubleday, 2008).

The Sin Eater's Workbook

THE FOLLOWING EXERCISES are offered if you would like to try some of the techniques and approaches in this book. There is no particular order in which these exercises must be followed.

❧❖ CLOUD GATHERING

Chapter two concerns the practice of taking guidance from nature, which relies on our surrender to chance and destiny. In its simplest form, it means holding a question in mind and walking out into the fields and forests with a desire only to be led by the whispers of spirit. The flight of birds across a valley, the play of sunlight on leaves, or even a gust of wind might then become significant and provide the answers we are looking for, since, as Adam put it, "nature is the visible face of spirit: a way of connecting with intelligent forces who know far more than we do."

Cloud gathering, or cloud gazing, is a traditional method of Celtic divination. To try it for yourself, find a quiet place in nature on a sunny day when there are also clouds in the sky. Lie on your back and close your eyes, then ask the question (out loud if you wish) that you are seeking an answer to.

Open your eyes and "gather" the first cloud you see. Study it, making a note of its shape, the way it moves, its size, density, texture, and so on. What does it remind you of or seem to be saying?

Adam taught that it is best to look for three signs—or, rather, to allow these signs to find you—so you can check the information each provides against the others and then creatively assemble all three to reveal a final answer. So repeat this exercise two more times in exactly the same way, and when you have finished, use your creative imagination to develop a story or theme that unites all of the guidance you have received.

The story you create is the answer to your question and your gateway to the future. It doesn't need to be a work of great poetry or even make rational sense. Your soul will understand its meaning.

◆ ◆ ◆

❧ WALKING A DRAGON PATH

"What is a dragon path?" Cad asks in chapter three. "There are many answers to that question ... but really they are threads of energy that link one place or soul to another.

"Beneath everything we know—or think we know— there is a web of energy that holds our reality together and exists beyond the visible world. A dragon path is a particular thread in that web that will lead us to someone or something—a place, a person, or a passage in time—with which we have some business because we share something in common: a mood or a taste or, more likely, a sacred purpose."

To explore the dragon paths in your own life, look for coincidences or synchronicities—things that link you in some intangible way with another person or place and that may also come in threes ("The hallmark of a good omen," according to Adam).

Perhaps you are reading a book, for example, and a place name leaps out at you. It may be somewhere you've never thought about before, but suddenly now its romance or intrigue starts to call you. Then, later that day, there is a television documentary about the same place, or a newspaper article, or a friend arrives unexpectedly and starts talking about it, unaware that it is on your mind too. Such events are more common than we think and signal a world opening up to us and beginning to let slip its secrets.

A dragon path now exists between that place and you, and to follow it may be to embark on a pilgrimage of your own to discover what hidden knowledge is there for you to find. Invariably, your life will change if you choose to make this journey.

◆ ◆ ◆

❖ An Experiment with Time

"Are you familiar with the works of John Dunne?" asks Cad in chapter four. "Some years ago, Mr. Dunne ... began to have dreams of events yet to happen, which, on waking, he found either to *be* real, or he would observe reality change over the next days and weeks until the events he had dreamed of *became* real ...

"And so Mr. Dunne began to wonder about the nature of a world where things like this could happen. Certainly, it was not the world that we are taught to believe in ... but one where future, past, and present are a single moment, eternal and swirling about us in an infinite and ongoing Now ... a world where distinctions of time are no more than descriptions of the mind and bear little resemblance to what is actually real ... [instead] in sleep, dreams, and reveries, our souls wander freely and make contact with other dimensions."

Dunne's experiment with time was really an exercise in lucid dreaming: the willful creation of a dream-state where we receive information from the world of spirit about events, people, places, or circumstances that may be distant from us in space or time as we perceive them but are ever-present when we enter a shamanic state of consciousness.

To begin lucid dreaming, make sure you are relaxed, and before you sleep, set yourself a task to visit a person or place and gather information about a possible future that relates to a subject you have in mind. Then sleep normally but set your alarm for a time a little different from normal (about three hours into your sleeping cycle is usually good), and, as soon as you wake, write down your thoughts, recollections, and intuitions about the person or place you have chosen or the event you have seen.

The next step is to watch for similar events in "real life"—and to realize from this that reality is not as fixed or certain as we may think and that time, if it exists at all, is not linear but always "now" in some other dimension of our dreaming.

♦ ♦ ♦

❧ "Stop!"

To bring the soul back to balance and return it to its natural order, "we began a sort of physical work where we would run through forests, wade rivers, climb trees ... aware that at any moment one of us could yell *stop*," says Cad in chapter six. "Immediately then we had to end what we were doing and hold ourselves in perfect pitch, even if we were clinging to the high branches of a tree or perching on a rock above a waterfall."

The Stop exercise is one to practice with a partner. Individually, you or the person you are working with will begin some activity—running, climbing, reading, thinking, meditating, gardening, painting ... it doesn't really matter what. At a certain point into this practice, the inactive partner gives the other an instruction to stop.

At this, the active partner ceases what he is doing and pays attention to his body, emotions, and thoughts, noting how he feels and where his mind has taken him.

The next stage is to track these thoughts, feelings, and sensations back to where they came from. You may be thinking (consciously or otherwise) of a job interview that is coming up, for example.

Level 1: How do you feel about it (excited, nervous, worried, etc.)?

Level 2: When have you felt like this before?

Level 3: What activities or circumstances unite the situations in which you have felt or feel this way?

Level 4: When was the first time these feelings ever arose—and in response to what?

And so on.

In this way, the Stop exercise begins to reveal our habitual thought processes and emotional reactions so we can bring them back under our control. We can then align our energies to our purpose instead of wasting them or falling victim to habits.

"It sounds simple," said Cad, "but through its practice, we learned a great deal about ourselves and strengthened our resolve to become men of destiny."

✦ ✦ ✦

❦ "I Am That Which I Am"

"Our final practice was a movement technique," says Cad, in chapter six. It looked and felt like tai chi. The moves were completed slowly in a continuous and gently flowing rhythm that began with us standing quite still and facing the sun, feeling its warmth as well as the breeze on our skin and, with eyes closed, listening to the sounds of nature with relaxed awareness to bring ourselves into balance. Our arms were then extended to the sides at shoulder height and, with eyes now open, we twisted at the waist, turning left and then right, as if to look directly behind us.

Through an act of visualization and tuning in to the environment, this movement enables you to draw power and awareness from the air, as if your fingers are antennae receiving wisdom from the world around you.

The next movement is to bend your knees, keeping your back straight, and to extend your fingers downwards until they touch the ground, so you absorb the power of the earth in the same way as the air. Then, standing upright, your arms are raised above your head to allow the energy of the earth to cascade over you and to receive the power of the sun.

Finally, your arms are brought to the sides and your body returns to its first position. The movement ends with an affirmation, spoken aloud: "I am that which I am."

A daily practice of this movement not only wakes up the body, mind, and spirit, but is a reminder of our place in the world:

> *I am me;*
> *I am not you.*
> *I take responsibility for myself*
> *While honoring your right to be.*
> *With that realization and caveat,*
> *I care for and express myself*
> *As I will.*

◆ ◆ ◆

❧ The Pilgrim's Way

While there are many "official" pilgrimage routes (such as that of Santiago de Compostela, which Cad describes in chapter seven), in fact, as Adam says: "Any action we make might be a pilgrimage, whether the journey takes a moment or a lifetime—because we are always acting ... To be pilgrims is what we came to this world to do. It is our destiny."

To undertake a pilgrimage requires, in this sense, only mindfulness: an "otherworldly" mindfulness, where we set our intentions and are led by intuition. Even a country walk or a trip to the shops can become a pilgrimage, then, because we are open to guidance from the world of spirit around us, beyond our normal concerns and agendas.

Wherever you are going and whatever you are doing today, slow down and walk at the pace of nature. Observe and look around you. Slow your breathing. Be part of the world.

Set yourself an intention that you are on a spiritual quest to use your journey as a way to deepen into spirit and increase your connection to nature. When you reach your destination, look for the signs that will answer you.

Even a supermarket can become a shrine of knowledge if you use your intention in this way and pay attention to the world.

◆ ◆ ◆

❧ The Vesica Piscis

Fittingly, in chapter eight I arrive at the Chalice Well in Glastonbury, which is protected by an oak and iron cover decorated by the ancient symbol of the vesica piscis: an elaborate figure eight dissected by the magical sword of King Arthur.

The figure eight, or lemniscate, was also the pilgrim's mark used by Adam and, as Cad explained it, a symbol of protection and security since it returns upon itself, leading away from and then back to the center: the place we have come from and return to on our travels. Through its use, therefore, "no pilgrim can ever lose himself."

Another of the moving meditations Cad taught me also uses this symbol. Its purpose is to still the mind and allow our spirits to flow so they blend with that of the wider universe.

Walk slowly, tracing an imaginary numeral eight on the ground as you walk. Breathe deeply and free your mind from everyday matters and concerns. Simply walk the labyrinth of the lemniscate.

It is good to start (and end) the day like this. By walking the eight for fifteen minutes or so, you will experience stillness, and your spiritual resources will be gathered around you so that any concerns you have can be viewed from a bigger and more central perspective and are no longer overwhelming. It is also an excellent prelude to lucid dreaming.

◆ ◆ ◆

❧ The Oaken Giants: A Tree Meditation

"Almost without thinking, I sank to the ground and sat cross-legged before the trees, drawn into a meditation. My eyes became unfocused, and I found myself gazing at the trees, dreaming myself into them and the evolution of the world that they had watched and been part of ... I was one with the memory of the trees, flowing like water through their season-rings and merging with the history contained there. I saw, as they had, the people who had made their prayers and offerings, and I knew what they longed for."

In chapter nine, I describe my encounter with Gog and Magog, the great oaks of Glastonbury. Although my own meditation was, in this instance, spontaneous and unplanned, it is possible to receive great wisdom from trees in a more deliberately meditative way.

It begins with slowing down and, as much as possible, losing yourself to nature. In this dreamlike state, find a tree you are drawn to and sit with your back against it. Close your eyes and allow yourself to dream more deeply so you make a spiritual and emotional, as well as a physical, connection to the tree you have chosen.

Trees, especially the great oaks, have been on Earth far longer than we have, and it may therefore be that, through the dreaming connection you make, a great deal of wisdom is offered to you in the form of ideas or thoughts that pop into your head or the feelings or body sensations that arise.

Don't dismiss it. Think about it, and you may find that the counsel you receive is exactly what you need to hear, even though it came from a source beyond the "normal" world.

◆ ◆ ◆

❧ The Oracle

In chapter ten, I write about an otherworldly encounter with Adam and the oracle he refers to as the Maid of the Hill:

"He led me to the end of the cave where, in the center, a throne of carved oak was standing on a stage before a curtain of red velvet. A woman dressed completely in white sat there unmoving, a veil draped over her head so that her face could not be seen. Beneath her oaken throne, a bowl of sage and bay leaves smouldered, surrounding her with aromatic smoke."

The appearance of the oracle and the words she spoke seem curious, but such is the way of oracles. The oracle priestesses of Delphi (also known as the Pythia, or Pythonesses) were the channels for Apollo, the god of light, sun, truth, medicine, healing, and poetry. They were usually older women, chosen from the peasants of the area, who had led a blameless and sin-free life. They sat on tripod thrones over an opening in the earth from which intoxicating fumes arose, so they fell into a trance where Apollo could possess them, and from him their prophecies would flow. Often they spoke in poetry or riddles, which were interpreted by the priests of the temple. Always their faces were hidden.

Such practices, therefore, have history to them, and it is as well to follow them if you wish to become an oracle, or Pythia, for others.

Cover your face and place a bowl of smoking sage and bay beneath you. Inhale deeply and begin to speak in a poetic stream of consciousness. Your words are for interpretation later. For now, let the spirits speak through you.

◆ ◆ ◆

❧ Good and Bad Seeds

How we know sin and how we avoid it are the questions posed in Adam's journal, which I write about in chapter twelve. For Adam, the answer was straightforward: "Pay attention to our actions and the results they produce." Then, "sooner or later we will learn what is useful for us and what impoverishes our souls …

"The good gardener plants good seeds and tends to them so they grow strong in the sunlight and add their beauty to the world."

In a sense, knowing sin (and avoiding it for the good of our souls) is trial and error, but "good gardeners" are shrewd. They test their actions in "the field of deeds" that is our world and, more importantly, they learn from them.

Not many people are good gardeners but rather, as the stranger explained it, are led by habits and conditioning so that only "five of twenty of twenty" will break the cycle of planting bad seeds and expecting nourishment from them.

Observe yourself. Keep a journal if you need to. Practice for yourself a sort of Stop exercise and record your thoughts, feelings, and responses and the outcomes they produce. Look back over it from time to time and you will become clearer on what are the good and bad seeds for you.

What is required next is purpose: a willful decision to act differently so that better outcomes result. This is the planting of good seeds—those which make the world more shiny and beautiful for you and others. Then we can lead lives "without regrets."

This Path of Purpose is not an easy one to follow, even though it is all we really have. So remember to forgive yourself for your errors as well. Then learn from them and try again. This is how the evolution of the soul—and the world—takes place.

◆ ◆ ◆

A Note
from the Author

Ｌᴉᴋᴇ ᴍʏ ꜰɪʀꜱᴛ book in this series, *The Sin Eater's Last Confessions*, *Walking with the Sin Eater* is offered as a work of semi-fiction, a narrative which describes in story form events and practices that are true and people who existed and, in some cases, continue to exist.

Specifically, there is (or was) a Cad (short for Cadwallader, a name that in Welsh means "leader of the battle"), just as there is (or was) an Adam, a sin eater who was born in Wales and whom I met in the Herefordshire village of Ullingswick during my childhood (a story told in *The Sin Eater's Last Confessions*). There was also a Melanie who owned a guesthouse in Glastonbury and still does so, whom I met in the way I described.

The myths and legends of Britain presented in this book, including the connections in Glastonbury and Wales to King Arthur, Jesus, and the Grail are also accurate, and these days, thanks to films like *The Da Vinci Code*, some of them are well known.

Finally, it is true that the journey at the heart of this book took place and is one of many pilgrimages I have now undertaken, for, as Adam writes, "there are many times when a pilgrimage may be useful to settle the mind and restore the soul." Nowadays, however, my annual pilgrimage is to the mountains and jungles of Peru to work with the shamans there and experience the magic of their teacher plants, ayahuasca and San Pedro.

Still, I cannot say that this book is entirely true because, once again, it has been written from the perspective of a grown man looking back on the events and undertakings of a child, so I have had to journey back in my imagination to reconnect with my thoughts and feelings then.

This, I suppose, is the way it is for all of us, for as the philosopher Søren Kierkegaard wrote, "Life can only be understood backwards" although "it must be *lived* forwards." With this looking backwards we also reinvent ourselves, so we continually create, re-create, and "update" the story of our lives, which we invent anew each day to help us make sense of the world. It is for this reason, if no other, that I offer this book as semi-fiction.

The word semi-fiction, however, implies, of course, that it is also semi-fact, and certainly the spiritual exercises I present here are valid and verifiable through your own practice. I teach many of them in the workshops I run.

It is these—the practices more than the story—which are important, since, as Adam wrote, "We must put our faith in what sings to us and in the places where truth can be found"—in our own experience, that is, rather than the words of others, because "what is truly sacred is a matter for each human heart to discover."

To be pilgrims is what we came to this world to do. I wish you the love and luck you deserve on your journey.

Ross Heaven
Brighton, January 2009

Index

Get the latest information on our body, mind, and spirit products! To receive a **free** copy of Llewellyn's consumer catalog, *New Worlds of Mind & Spirit,* simply call 1-877-NEW-WRLD or visit our website at www.llewellyn.com and click on *New Worlds.*

LLEWELLYN ORDERING INFORMATION

Order Online:
Visit our website at www.llewellyn.com, select your books, and order them on our secure server.

Order by Phone:
- Call toll-free within the U.S. at 1-877-NEW-WRLD (1-877-639-9753). Call toll-free within Canada at 1-866-NEW-WRLD (1-866-639-9753)
- We accept VISA, MasterCard, and American Express

Order by Mail:
Send the full price of your order (MN residents add 6.875% sales tax) in U.S. funds, plus postage & handling to:

> **Llewellyn Worldwide**
> **2143 Wooddale Drive, Dept. 978-0-7387-1916-0**
> **Woodbury, MN 55125-2989**

Postage & Handling:
Standard (U.S., Mexico & Canada). If your order is:
    $24.99 and under, add $4.00
    $25.00 and over, FREE STANDARD SHIPPING

AK, HI, PR: $16.00 for one book plus $2.00 for each additional book.

International Orders (airmail only):
    $16.00 for one book plus $3.00 for each additional book

Orders are processed within 2 business days.
Please allow for normal shipping time.
Postage and handling rates subject to change.

THE SIN EATER'S LAST CONFESSIONS
Lost Traditions of Celtic Shamanism

Ross Heaven

Considered a madman in his English village, Adam Dilwyn Vaughan—a sin eater—was shunned by the same community who flocked to him for healing. This true tale records Ross Heaven's fascinating journey as the sin eater's apprentice, who is introduced to the lost art of sin eating and other Celtic shamanic traditions.

This spiritual memoir records the author's wondrous, moving experiences with the powerful energies of the natural world. He witnesses Adam removing negative energies from a patient, discovers his soul purpose through dreaming, goes on a vision quest in a sacred cave, and participates in a sin-eating ritual. Interlacing these remarkable events are Welsh legends and enlightening discussions that shed light on these mysterious practices and invite you to see the world through the eyes of a shaman. Also included is a sin eater's workbook of the same shamanic exercises and techniques practiced by Adam.

978-0-7387-1356-4 • 5 x 7, 288 pp. • bibliog., index • $16.95

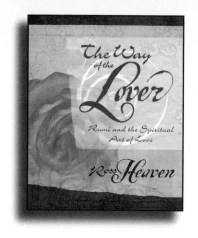

THE WAY OF THE LOVER
Rumi and the Spiritual Art of Love

Ross Heaven

The revered words of Jalaluddin Rumi—the greatest love poet of all time—have endured for centuries. His moving verses can help us answer life's greatest questions: What is true love? How can I be more loving? How can love help me grow spiritually?

Drawing on Rumi's writings, Sufi teachings, and shamanic techniques, Ross Heaven presents an utterly unique spiritual guidebook to love and relationships. Your voyage through every stage of the soul is aided by the Medicine Wheel, a spiritual compass that will guide you on "The Path of the Heart." Use this powerful tool to revitalize relationships, uncover fears, resist self-defeating impulses, recover from depression or "soul fatigue," and master the "Art of Love."

978-0-7387-1117-1 • 7 1/2 x 9 1/8, 216 pp. • bibliog., index • $16.95

VA-VA-VOODOO
Find Love, Make Love & Keep Love

Kathleen Charlotte
Foreword by Ross Heaven

How many professional therapists can put together a powerful mojo bag or an intoxicating love perfume to attract a mate? As a relationship counselor and a Voodoo initiate, Kathleen Charlotte offers the best of both worlds in her refreshing, witty, and magical guide to this crazy little thing called love.

Va-Va-Voodoo introduces five key Voodoo lwa, or "angels," including Baron, the spirit who loves spicy rum and cigars, and La Sirène, an ocean goddess of seduction and sensuality. Readers learn how to "feed the spirits" and request their help in attracting a lover, finding "the one," keeping a relationship steamy, or recovering from heartbreak. A perfect blend of practical magic and inspiring, down-to-earth advice, this one-of-a-kind book includes magic rituals, charms, aphrodisiacs, and spells, as well as helpful relationship tips regarding communication, self-esteem, intimacy, sex, break-ups, and forgiveness.

978-0-7387-0994-9 • 7 x 7, 168 pp. • $14.95

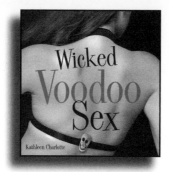

WICKED VOODOO SEX

Kathleen Charlotte

Kathleen Charlotte invites women to become "spiritual sluts" and embrace the powerful healing essence of sex—Voodoo style. Provocative and unapologetically candid, this saucy sex guide offers Voodoo-Tantric practices that will invigorate your sex life and enrich your sexual power.

Flirt like a goddess. Transform your bedroom into a temple of love. Invite Voodoo spirits to take possession during lovemaking. Take a tour of the erogenous zones and discover new ways to stimulate them. By reveling in sex as a holy, healing, and wholesome activity, you'll dispel sexual shame and awaken powerful goddess energy vital to health and happiness.

Sexual positions, Voodoo trance, astral sex, aphrodisiacs, magic spells, erotic dance, and sexual healing rituals are all covered in this bold and bawdy collection of Voodoo sex secrets.

978-0-7387-1200-0 • 7 x 7, 264 pp. • $16.95

SHAMANISM FOR BEGINNERS

*Walking with the World's
Healers of Earth and Sky*

James Endredy

Interest in shamanism is on the rise, and people are eager to integrate this intriguing tradition into their own lives. *Shamanism for Beginners* introduces the spiritual beliefs and customs of the shaman—a spiritual leader, visionary, healer, diviner, walker between worlds, and so much more.

How is one called to be a shaman? How is a shaman initiated? Where does a shaman's power come from? Exploring the practices and beliefs of tribes around the world, James Endredy sheds light on the entire shamanic experience. The fascinating origins and evolution of shamanism are examined, along with power places, tools (costume, drum, sweat lodge, medicine wheel), sacred plants, and the relationship between the shaman and spirits. Enriched with the author's personal stories and quotes from actual shaman elders and scholars, Endredy concludes with incredible feats of shamans, healing techniques, and ruminations on the future of this remarkable tradition.

978-0-7387-1562-9 • 5³⁄₁₆ x 8, 288 pp. • $14.95

THE RUMI TAROT KIT

Nigel Jackson

Tread the sacred path of the Sufi and wander through the garden of divine love with *The Rumi Tarot Kit*. Considered one of the greatest saints, teachers, and writers of the Sufi tradition, Rumi extolled love and its ability to set the soul to flight. This mystical and contemplative tarot invites you to seek your own spiritual bliss.

Rich with Eastern opulence, the symbolic imagery in each card depicts the soul's upward journey toward ultimate truth and features an inspirational verse from the popular mystic and poet. See the Fool, the Emperor, the Empress, and other familiar figures in flowing robes surrounded by swirling skies. Use this deck to enhance your spiritual practice through divination, meditation, visualization, and chanting.

Also included is a guidebook that explains the meanings of each card within the Major and Minor Arcana, gives suggested card layouts, and presents a fascinating biographical overview of Rumi and historical background of the Sufi tradition.

978-0-7387-1168-3 • $28.95 • Boxed kit includes a 78-card deck, a 312-page book (5³/₁₆ x 8), and a black pouch

ECOSHAMANISM
Sacred Practices of Unity, Power and Earth Healing

James Endredy

In a society riddled with rampant consumerism and unsustainable technology, it's easy for everyone, including shamans, to lose touch with the natural world. James Endredy, who has learned from tribal shamans around the globe, presents a new philosophy of shamanic practice called ecological shamanism, or ecoshamanism. Designed to deliver well-being and spiritual harmony, ecoshamanism is the culmination of the visionary practices, rituals, and ceremonies that honor and support nature.

Exploring the holistic perspective of shamanism, Endredy encourages readers to establish a rewarding connection with sacred, life-giving forces using shamanic tools and practices. The author describes more than fifty authentic ecoshamanistic practices—including ceremonies, rituals, chanting, hunting, pilgrimage, and making instruments—that reinforce one's relationship with the natural world.

978-0-7387-0742-6 • 7¹/₂ x 9 ¹/₈, 360 pp. • $19.95

To Write to the Author

If you wish to contact the author or would like more information about this book, please write to the author in care of Llewellyn Worldwide and we will forward your request. Both the author and the publisher appreciate hearing from you and learning of your enjoyment of this book and how it has helped you. Llewellyn Worldwide cannot guarantee that every letter written to the author can be answered, but all will be forwarded. Please write to:

Ross Heaven
℅ Llewellyn Worldwide
2143 Wooddale Drive, Dept. 978-0-7387-1916-0
Woodbury, MN 55125-2989

Please enclose a self-addressed stamped envelope for reply,
or $1.00 to cover costs. If outside U.S.A., enclose
international postal reply coupon.

Many of Llewellyn's authors have websites with additional information and resources. For more information, please visit our website:

HTTP://WWW.LLEWELLYN.COM